the Lord will say why did you steal that book

Steal not this book for fear of shame for in it is the owners name for if you do

away and if you say you do not know the Lord will say go down below.

# This book belongs ~to~

IVY ALLCOCK

216 PEARTREE AVE

SOUTHAMPTON.

~~~ Ex Libris ~~~

# SUSSEX VILLAGES

# Sussex Villages

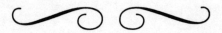

MICHAEL H. C. BAKER

*Photographs by the author*

ROBERT HALE · LONDON

Robert Hale Limited
Clerkenwell House
Clerkenwell Green
London EC1R 0HT

Printed in Great Britain by
Clarke, Doble & Brendon Ltd.
Plymouth and London

# Contents

To
Maeve, William and Daniel
who helped

# Illustrations

The main street at Mayfield
Rotherfield
Choir practice in Worth church
Hartfield during a March snowstorm

*Map pages 14 and 15*
This map is based with permission on the Ordnance Survey.

# 1

# The Changing Village

WE all once lived in villages and retain some inherited instinct which directs us to re-creating a village-like community, a fairly small group of people, each offering a basic skill or service or, just as important, a familiar face and a helping hand when it is needed. An apparently featureless suburb or factory-built tower block may well encompass an intricate and carefully evolved series of relationships only dimly discernible to the outsider. It might therefore be argued that a large town is in reality a number of villages grouped together and that the various districts of Brighton —Kemp Town, Seven Dials, Preston Park, for example—ought to be included in this book. Clearly this is not what the reader expects and would be at variance with the *Oxford English Dictionary* definition of a village which is a "place smaller than a town, where there are houses and shops and usually a church and school". But it is worth bearing in mind that the differences between town and village life are not as great as might be imagined.

If we take another look at the dictionary definition of a village we see that although it quite obviously rules out Brighton and the other resorts and inland towns such as Crawley and Horsham, it is a good deal less helpful when it comes to a place like Wadhurst or Bramber where there are houses, shops, a school and a church and much else; but is the "much else" sufficient to elevate a large village into a small town? And at the other end of the scale, what is the difference between a small village and a hamlet?

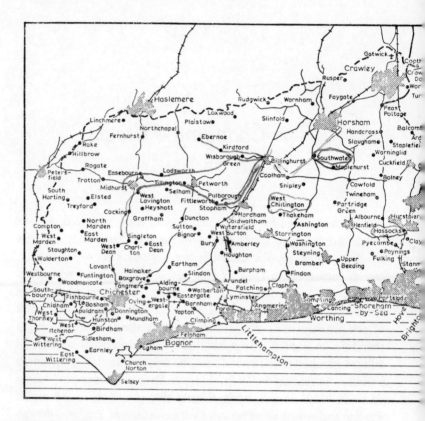

There are no clear-cut answers. Area and population give us some guidance and I don't think we can allow anywhere without some form of church to call itself a village, although the possession of one doesn't mean it cannot be a hamlet. A village ought to have a public house, a junior school and at least one shop, although Withyham, for example, does not possess the latter but is nevertheless quite certainly more substantial than a hamlet. And subsidized school buses have meant that adjacent villages nowadays often share a school or send their children to a nearby town. One might imagine that the inhabitants would be the best judge of the status of where they live, but this is not always so. Old people sometimes do not take into account the many changes which may

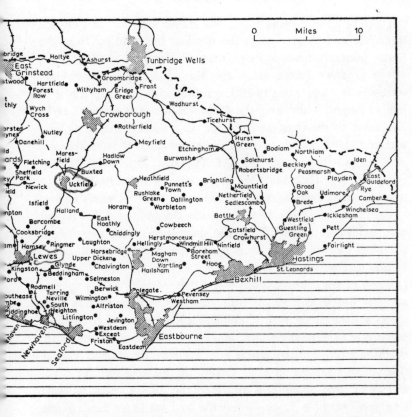

have occurred since they were young and they still see their community as it was fifty or more years ago; others do not have sufficient knowledge of other places to make a sound judgement. I was once assured by a resident of Kirdford that nearby Petworth was a village, which it surely cannot be; in the Wadhurst parish magazine there is a section with the heading "Town in Focus", whilst on the opposite page is a reference to "the quiet village". Ultimately it is all a matter of opinion and I have included villages which I am sure some will regard as either hamlets or towns, whilst I have no doubt left out one or two which it will be argued should be in.

Sussex is one of the more populous English counties, the total

population in 1977 being 1,278,000. Administratively it is divided
into East and West Sussex, the dividing line running from the
Surrey border just east of East Grinstead, along the western fringes
of the Ashdown Forest, across the Bluebell Railway, east of Haywards Heath and Burgess Hill, parallel with the Brighton line,
behind Brighton and over the Downs south of the Devil's Dyke
and down to the coast at Portslade. East Sussex, with a population of 652,000, covers an area in excess of 530,000 acres; the area
of West Sussex, population 625,000, is a little over 402,000
acres. In 1801 the population of the county was 190,000, when
it sent twenty-eight MPs to Westminster; today it sends twelve.

Unlike much of the rest of Britain the Industrial Revolution
only indirectly accounted for the great rise in the population;
the chief reason was a book by Dr Richard Russell of Lewes
called A Dissertation Concerning the Use of Sea Water in
Diseases of the Glands, which was published in 1750. Its appearance happened to coincide with an upsurge of interest in such
matters amongst the general public. Dr Russell moved to the fishing village of Brighthelmston, and the seaside holiday was born.
Brighton's transformation was confirmed by the visit of George
III's younger brother in 1765 and by the Prince Regent in 1783,
and from then on villages all along the Sussex coast followed
Brighton's example. Some—where the land was in the hands of one
family—grew in a fairly orderly manner, others developed according to the speculative builder's fancy. Those villages which
initially escaped the attention of the holidaymaker and the day-
tripper later found themselves absorbed by an expanding neighbour and by World War II there was scarcely a village clearly
recognizable as such left between Bognor and Seaford.

Inland the changes were much less dramatic and as late as the
first decade of the present century, more than fifty years after the
railway had come to Sussex, many village people lived lives little
different in essentials from those lived in medieval times. In the
words of Leonard Woolf in Beginning Again, "Conditions in Sussex
in 1912 were pretty primitive, and our daily life was probably

nearer that of Chaucer's than of the modern man". Even today the contrast between seaside Sussex and those villages away from the main traffic arteries is great. Indeed when one considers how near to London and how popular is the Sussex coast the remarkable thing is not how greatly the country has been despoiled but how much remains untouched.

Almost all Sussex villages date back to Saxon times, as their names indicate. Any village with an *ly* or *ley* ending, e.g. Amberley, Hellingly, Ardingly, is likely to be found inland and was once a meadow or a clearing; it is not to be confused with an *ey* ending which is the Anglo-Saxon for island, as Selsey or the lost hamlet of Horseye on the Pevensey Marshes. *Ham*, as in Burpham, Sidlesham or Magham Down, means a settlement, as does *ing*—Clymping, Patching, Guestling—whilst *mer* signifies the presence of water. The latter is almost the same as the modern *mere*, and indeed if Keymer is pronounced in a Sussex accent one gets something very close to Cowmere—the drinking place of the cows. Although the greatest of the Anglo-Saxons, King Alfred, had his capital some ten miles across the Hampshire border at Winchester, he owned many manors in Sussex, out of which have grown, amongst others, the villages of West Dean, Barnham and Ditchling, and his father, Ethelwulf, was buried at Steyning. No complete building from Alfred's time remains in the county but it is nevertheless true that the Sussex of his time and of ours is recognizably the same. Certainly not the Sussex of Bognor, Brighton or Eastbourne, nor of Crawley or Burgess Hill, but in the villages of the Downs and the Weald the old outlines and patterns remain and can be seen.

The greatest threat to this pattern came neither with the development of the seaside nor the arrival of the railway. The former certainly destroyed it within the immediate vicinity of the coastline, aided by the latter; elsewhere, apart from isolated examples in the vicinity of the junctions at Haywards Heath, Barnham, Three Bridges and Polegate, the railway merely exposed the threat.

For most Sussex village men their first real experience of the

B

outside world came with the First World War. For many it was also their last and in every village a memorial—a cross, a tablet on a wall or a hall or some improvement to the village green—records the names of those who died. The war was very close to Sussex and George Aitchison wrote in November 1918, "I crossed the common at Chailey during the height of our first Somme attack and was startled with the thunder of the guns. The very earth was vibrating." The reality of the phrase "The Lost Generation" can never sink to mere cliché for anyone who has read the thousands of names commemorated throughout Sussex. The wonder is that there were any young men left at all in 1918; at Ticehurst, for example, eleven former employees of the village store alone gave their lives.

The war gave a great boost to the internal combustion engine, and the motor car, the lorry and the bus which first appeared on Sussex roads around the turn of the century multiplied and became commonplace. The farmworker and his family who had previously to walk for perhaps several hours to reach the nearest town—unless they happened to live near a railway station—and therefore seldom undertook such an expedition, now found a Southdown bus would get them there in a matter of minutes. Their horizons broadened enormously. At the same time the wireless was beginning and there was education for all, if only up to a fairly elementary level.

Whether everyone got the education for which he or she was fitted is another question. The Vicar of Maynards Green complained at this time that the modern curriculum often took no account of the ways of country children. In a letter to the *Sussex County Magazine* he commended the local school on its bee club and he remarked that watching and looking after the bees made "rough boys gentle". It was not until after World War II that most country children received full secondary education; in 1934 there were 20,565 children in West Sussex in elementary schools and only 2,200 in secondary ones, of which there were eight. £259,000 was spent on elementary education, £80,000 on higher education.

At this time there were still a number of very small village schools with less than fifty pupils each, one or two in fact with less than a dozen and these were being closed. There were also, of course, many fee-paying schools in Sussex, as there are today, but these were no concern of village children. The Rev. A. A. Evans, Vicar of East Dean and Friston from 1908 to 1929, was one who felt unhappy about the new developments in education. He remarked that "For 10 years I have never heard of a case of truancy in our village school" and he feared that country children who went to school in town would forget country ways. Evans was no sentimentalist about village life and he complained bitterly that the farmhand was "the worst-paid man in the land; no unemployment dole, when that comes, is for him—only the cold charity of the officials of the Guardians". Few farmworkers had any annual holiday before 1939.

Evans's *On Foot in Sussex*, published in 1933, is one of the best books on the county, but probably his most perceptive work appeared in the *Sussex County Magazine* for which he wrote over a long period. Anyone wishing to recapture the authentic feel of village and country—and town—life in all its fascinating detail should consult this work, which was published every month from 1926 until July 1956. Fortunately a number of public libraries in the county have complete, or almost complete, sets of it. Its founder and first editor was Arthur Beckett, a Yorkshireman who came to Sussex at the age of fourteen when his father took over the *Eastbourne Gazette*.

I talked to one of his former employees, Mr Ravenshield, who still works for the *Gazette* and who remembered him and Evans with affection. He told me that the *Magazine* was Beckett's hobby and his chief interest and when he died it was kept going as a tribute to him. Despite the quality of its writing and the fascination of its subject matter the magazine attracted barely sufficient advertising and it never really recovered from the restrictions and the drop in circulation during the Second World War. In the end it was losing £1,000 a year and when its closure was announced

*The Times* was one of many national newspapers which regretted its passing. It wrote that it was "perhaps the oldest—and some would say the best—of the County periodicals". It has left a gap which has never been filled.

Life in a Sussex village was never less than hard, although how hard depended on the general state of the economy. When it was very bad, as in the years immediately after the Napoleonic Wars, starvation was common and led to uprisings. The average wage was between 7s. and 8s. *a* week which was totally inadequate, and under duress employers agreed to double this, but few actually did so. Fifty-two of those agitating for better conditions were brought to trial at Chichester, one was executed, seventeen were transported, sixteen jailed. Cobbett saw things differently. He admitted that the wages of village labourers were low but when he rode through the county in the early 1820s he saw "no wretchedness in Sussex; nothing at all to be compared to that which I have seen in other parts. There is an appearance of comfort about the dwellings of the labourers. The houses are good and warm". Yet a Sussex parish priest wrote in 1830, "Many of the cottages of this village are unfit for housing pigs", and he presumably was a good deal better acquainted with conditions than Cobbett.

In many parts of Britain the enclosure of land had a dramatic and disastrous effect on country people, but in Sussex it was a far more gradual process, beginning soon after the Conquest. It nevertheless was often resisted and in the latter part of Henry VIII's reign there were riots at Waldron, Laughton and East Hoathly when enclosures were destroyed, fences burned down and animals taken out of the pound. The Dissolution did village people no service for many of the religious had employed them, supported them when out of work and cared for them when ill. Fortunately Tudor times saw a great revival in the iron industry and by the end of the sixteenth century it employed approximately one in ten of the male working population of the county. It is difficult today, when surveying the peaceful villages of the Weald, to imagine a time when they were at the heart of industrial England, yet such was their position during the reign of the first Elizabeth. It was, of course, on a vastly different scale from the Industrial Revolution which succeeded it. One could be quite familiar with the county and yet be unaware of its existence save for the telltale wisps of blue woodsmoke drifting skywards from the depths of the forest. It was very much a cottage industry. A furnace was a roughly made affair, easily demolished, and even the forges where the iron was shaped and manufactured were in many cases no larger than a village blacksmith's shop. The last working forge in Sussex, at Ashburnham, shut down in 1828 and today all that remains in most villages as a reminder of their industrial past is a stream flowing reddish brown, a woodland track paved with cinders from a long-vanished bloomery, a Forge Lane or a Furnace Cottage.

Sussex villages are renowned for their picturesqueness and their fine state of preservation. Within them are houses and cottages centuries old which are generally considered, along with the parish churches, their great glory. Yet Evans describes a Sussex village in the sixteenth century in the following terms: "The only things of charm and beauty would be the sky and the earth which God made, and the village church which men made . . . houses were more truly hovels, built of wattle, mud and thatch, one-roomed dwellings except for a loft. The floors were hard clay, and the fire was in the midst, with wreaths of wood smoke." A good many of these hovels survive, now transformed into architectural gems, but as far removed from their original state as is Brighton from Brighthelmston. A visit to the Downland Museum at Singleton provides a salutary reminder of just how primitive a medieval dwelling was, and how inward looking and isolated life in a Sussex village could be.

Until well into the present century a large proportion of the population of inland Sussex lived secluded, secretive, almost medieval lives in villages deep in the Wealden woodlands. They may nominally have been good members of the Church of England but their beliefs and customs were rooted in an older philosophy predating Saxons and Romans. Cold Comfort Farm is an exaggeration but it is not caricature. For many, drunkenness was the chief relaxation from long hours of work, as it had been for centuries, and this was as true of the doctor, the priest, the school-master and the squire as of the illiterate majority. Sussex was no better nor worse than the rest of England; the town dweller who imagines that strain and stress is something that came in with psychiatry has not looked beyond the superficial picturesqueness of village life and seen the narrowness and boredom often there beneath it.

Thomas Turner's Diary of East Hoathly, written in the mid-eighteenth century, is a catalogue of drunken orgies, always re-gretted the morning afterwards. In many of them the vicar plays a leading role and Turner himself was at one time the village school-master. Many of his roisterings are more comical than degrading, although this was not everyone's view, and John Wesley, who travelled a good deal through Sussex and preached his last open-air sermon at Winchelsea, found much amiss in rural communities. On one particular evening Turner got into bed drunk at 3 a.m., two hours before his wife, who eventually retired in a similar state. A short while later the vicar and some friends called, hauled Turner out of bed, persuaded him to perform a dance in his wife's petticoats, and finally departed at three o'clock in the afternoon.

The 1920s mark the period of the great change. The power of the big estates—whether beneficial or otherwise—was waning, although even today it is far from gone. Many of the big houses were taken over by successful industrialists, writers, entertainment personalities and cabinet ministers; the drift from the land which had been going on since the Industrial Revolution was accelerated by the increasing use of machinery on the land; the cottages vacated by the farmhands were put on the market by estate agents and snapped up by town dwellers as weekend homes; whilst, most important of all, the car brought the most remote of villages within an hour or so of London and the suburbs.

In 1934 the following letter from a native of Forest Row, returning after an absence of thirty-five years, was published in the *Sussex County Magazine.*

I was shocked and disgusted to see how the dear old countryside was being hopelessly defiled by the estate butchers, and defaced by the rawness and vile vulgarity of the speculative builder. No longer did I meet on the road the old Sussex yeoman in his slate-coloured elaborately yoked and frilled smock frock, and his buttoned-up hip leggings and heavy hobnailed boots.

That was one way of looking at it. Certainly there was little of beauty in the ribbon development of the 1920s and early 1930s and if it had been allowed to go on unchecked many villages would have been submerged and become mere suburbs or satellites of adjoining towns. There were also proposals for the construction of aerodromes in various parts of Sussex and three were built close together in the flat south-west of the county between the sea and the Downs by the RAF at Thorney Island, Tangmere and Ford. Shoreham had been in use as a civil aerodrome since 1910 and there had been an airship base at Polegate—of which one or two sheds remain—in World War I. In 1929 the Air Ministry approved the siting of three more aerodromes at Worthing, Bognor and Littlehampton, Brighton announced its intention to build an aerodrome on the Downs above Portslade, and a group of business-men proposed one on the Downs just above Friston on land about to be taken over by the National Trust.

But the dangers were seen. The West Sussex Town Planning Committee was set up in 1932 and laid down guidelines concern-ing development, overhead electric lines and advertisement hoard-ings, and following the Ribbon Development Act of 1935 which gave local authorities the right to impose restrictions on all classi-fied roads, East Sussex immediately applied it in full, while West Sussex applied it to 120 stretches of varying lengths. And in the event Shoreham remained the only commercial airport in Sussex, other than Gatwick which in any case until a few years ago belonged to Surrey.

Paradoxically had it not been for the development between the two world wars Sussex villages would hardly be in the fine state of preservation that they are today. The newcomers settled in Sussex because they appreciated its beauties, whilst those already there realized they must fight to preserve them. Sussex probably suffered less from the 1929 recession and the following slump than any other part of the country and its increasing prosperity reached out to the villages. Overhead power lines may be an eyesore, but if they brought light and warmth to farmhands and their families and an opening up to them of the outside world through the wireless, then it was a price worth paying. Only those who have never had to read by its insipid light, cope with its fumes or clean away the dirt it creates would consider an oil light romantic.

Health services improved too. As late as 1922 the Royal Sussex County Hospital at Brighton, which served the surrounding countryside, was so short of funds it had to close down 110 of its 225 beds. It was only able to reopen them the following year by means of a grant from the Voluntary Hospitals Commission. By 1937 things had improved to the extent that there were 100 District Nurses in East Sussex and 107 in West Sussex. They belonged to the Sussex Association of the Queen's Institute and were chiefly financed by the families they served, contributions per family ranging from 4s. 4d. to 8s. 8d. per year.

Certainly changing times meant the loss of some traditions. The smock had long been the standard dress for country people and within the one basic design boasted many variations, carters and woodmen each having embroidered devices whilst shepherds wore a piece of wool in their buttonholes and carters carried whips so that strangers at fairs would know their callings. The smock was usually worn with corduroy trousers which were of two sorts, the ordinary, light-coloured, small-webbed variety for labourers and the more dressy, gypsy-brown, large and small ribbed variety for skilled men. Until the end of the nineteenth century dog urine was used in their making. This was collected in iron bottles and sold to the manufacturers in the north of England. New trousers were hung out of the window for several nights to get rid of the smell, and it was said that a good frost helped. Corduroys, of the non-smelly variety, are of course worn today, but the smock began to give way to a shirt and jacket in the 1880s, and although it was still common at the time of the First World War, it had virtually gone by the Second.

Mechanization in the countryside slowly overtook the wind- and water-mill, and the horse and the ox. There were 200 working windmills in 1825, only 52 one hundred years later, and none in regular commercial use now, although a great many have been preserved, some in working order. There are few horses still used on farms in Sussex, but the last team of oxen was retired to the Pevensey Marshes from Exceat in 1925. In the latter part of the eighteenth century the dark red Sussex ox was considered the best breed in the country and, crossed with either Welsh or Herefords, was in universal use. Latterly it was used on the Downs where the treading of its cloven hoofs was very beneficial to the chalky soil. A horse was faster and more intelligent than an ox, although the latter was not stupid, and they might work together. An ox was stronger and a less fussy eater. It was broken in at the age of two and a half years, worked for five years, and then fattened for beef. The continuing use of animals and the absence of motor traffic ensured that most village streets were liberally strewn with dung until the 1920s.

Hop-picking is usually associated with Kent but it also goes on in East Sussex. Until the present century the hop-picking area extended a good deal further west than it does now—Thomas Turner writes of hop-pickers at Halland—and there are many villages in the East Grinstead, Uckfield and Hailsham areas which possess converted oast houses. East Londoners would come down for the picking, many of them emigrants, and a writer recalled in the *Sussex County Magazine* that the majority were of either German or Irish origin. The Germans lived in old railway carriages and were clean and quiet, whilst the Irish lived all together in a huge barn and were noisy and quarrelsome, "but more fun". Old inhabitants have suggested that it is the changing climate which has ended hop-picking in Sussex other than in the area bounded by Robertsbridge, Bodiam, the A21 and the Kent border, but it seems more likely that it was a reluctance to adopt modern methods and mechanization.

The Sussex village of today is likely to contain something from every century from the eleventh to the present and there may well be relics going back further. Inevitably, however ancient the exterior and the basic structure of a house or cottage, it is unlikely to lack the comforts of the twentieth century. Many of the inhabitants of Sussex villages are retired people, not native to the county—approximately half the people living in Sussex were born elsewhere—and there are some who would say that this has meant a loss of vitality, with too many young people leaving the villages for the towns. But it is these same elderly people who have ensured the preservation of much of Sussex. Whilst seldom wealthy they have usually been sufficiently well off to either restore or rebuild their houses and sufficiently community minded to care for the state of their village and the surrounding countryside. Often it is the farmhand who lives in the modern house and is glad to move to it from an ancient cottage with small windows, low beams and uneven floors. However picturesque its appearance a house is for living in and it is not everyone who can see the possibilities, possesses sufficient funds, or grasps the architectural essentials necessary for the preservation of a medieval building. Improvement is possibly a better word than preservation for a medieval building in its original state was a primitive affair, as can be judged by some of the exhibits at Singleton.

In most Sussex villages the church was restored, to either a lesser or greater degree, in Victorian times. It may not always have been done with sensitivity, but it often saved the church from dereliction. The most famous piece of restoration was Gilbert Scott's rebuilding of Chichester Cathedral spire in 1861. The original one collapsed in a spectacular manner and was a talking point in the county for months afterwards. It was weak and its collapse was fully expected. One of those who saw it happen was a man on duty in the semaphore tower in Portsmouth Dockyard. He was looking at it through his telescope and saw it disappear "like a concertina".

The most significant development in modern Sussex village life has been the acquisition by almost every household of a car. It has completed the opening up of the village to the outside world, and the outside world to it, a process which began with the coming of the railway and was continued by the bus. One of its effects has been to bring about the closure of many branch lines, and rural bus services are a shadow of their former selves. This is sad for there was something friendly, an extension of village life, about the local train, as there still is, to a degree, in the buses which still run. Now the great majority of rail services in Sussex are patronized by commuters, trippers and holiday-makers, and the buses chiefly by school children and old people.

But the benefits outweigh the losses, for the freedom offered by the car is unique. It is a freedom which can be easily abused and some main-road villages have lost more than they have gained. The first bypasses were built in the 1930s and have brought peace again to many villages. Building, both private and council, has gone on in most villages throughout the 1950s and 1960s and into the present decade, although on a decreasing scale and in a controlled manner. The Strategic Plan for the South-East, commissioned by the Government in 1968 and published in June 1970, foresees the greatest expansion in the Crawley/Burgess Hill area where there has already been an enormous amount of growth since World War II. Crawley has absorbed a number of villages and created others, although all form part of the town and are linked to each other. The changed economic situation has made it unlikely that the Plan's predictions will come about in their entirety, but Sussex remains, and is likely to remain almost the most popular county in England for visiting, for living in and for retiring to. The pressures on the village will certainly continue and will bring about changes, but this should not be a cause for regret. Some good things may go but others will take their place. Sussex village life remains vigorous, happily absorbing newcomers in a manner which would not have been possible in less enlightened days, yet at the same time preserving enough of the old to retain a sense of continuity.

## 2

## *Along the Surrey Border*

THIS chapter begins with a couple of false starts, Charlwood and Lowfield Heath. Under the local authority revisions of the early 1970s Charlwood, a handsome village one mile west of Gatwick Airport, was, like Gatwick, to be transferred from Surrey to West Sussex. The local inhabitants protested vehemently and although Charlwood did actually become a Sussex village for a year and is so marked on the current quarter-inch Ordnance Survey map, the protests were so effective that it was returned to Surrey. Lowfield Heath, like Gatwick Airport beside which it stands, became and has remained part of Sussex, but it has by now virtually ceased to be a village. Its inhabitants have dispersed, its houses have been demolished and replaced by industrial and other airport buildings and almost all that remains of the old village is the Victorian parish church of St Michael and All Angels and a wooden post mill without sweeps. Both are close to the main A23 London to Brighton road, but whilst the mill is in open country the poor old church stands amongst warehouses and within a hundred yards of jumbo jets thundering down the runway.

Rusper is our first village proper, three miles south-west of Charlwood and a half-mile beyond the Surrey border deep in the woods which cover the border country. It is a small village in terms of population although the parish encompasses 3,122 acres, a considerable area. Its name derives from the Saxon word for a rough enclosure in a forest; whilst there remain many trees in and around the village the roughness vanished long ago to be replaced by careful cultivation and neat gardens and hedgerows. Beside the village pub is a telephone exchange the size of a large bus shelter and next to that the recreation ground complete, like so many Sussex village greens, with swings, a slide and a see-saw.

Opposite is the church of St Mary Magdalene. I once came across a comment in the visitor's book, entered by Master T. Lawrence of Rusper, that it was "the best church in the World". As a resident he was probably better able to judge its qualities than those visitors who regard churches as merely pieces of architecture. The guidebook admits that from an architectural point of view its rebuilding in 1854–5 was "not entirely successful", but it was probably necessary. To quote W. S. Mitchell in a recent edition of the *Chichester News*: "In the mid-nineteenth century churches were in a deplorable condition", and an insensitive rebuilding which rendered the fabric waterproof and enabled worship to continue was of more use to the parishioners than a picturesque ruin. The famous piano-making family of Broadwood who actually lived in the adjoining Surrey parish of Capel were responsible for the rebuilding; the oldest part is the massive tower of 1489–1503. One of the many links with the Broadwoods is an attractive alabaster and marble memorial to Lucy Etheldred Broadwood, a pioneer of folk-song research, who died in 1929. Underneath one of the firs in the churchyard is a gravestone which reveals the history of a sad little family: the infant daughter died in 1916, the father was killed on the Western Front a year later, the mother lived on until 1950. One could become very melancholy studying inscriptions in village churchyards so it is as well to remind ourselves that they have seen revels as well as funerals. The churchyard has always been a handy spot for courting and in smuggling days an empty tomb made a good hiding place for contraband.

The assistant in the grocer's shop at Warnham has a broad Sussex accent which comes as rather a surprise, for superficially Warnham has the air of a garden suburb rather than that of a Sussex village. It lies in that area north of the Horsham–Crawley–

East Grinstead road which might as easily be Surrey as Sussex. The skies over Warnham are filled with the noise of aircraft landing at or taking off from Gatwick Airport, it has a station served by suburban trains which connect it with such places as Peckham Rye, Tulse Hill and Hackbridge, and it contains a great many recently erected houses of the sort found in Esher, Ham and Dulwich.

These modern developments have done Warnham no harm. They have ensured that it has retained a life of its own rather than looking to Horsham, two miles away, whilst at the same time the architects of each new group of houses, aware of the need to produce something in keeping with the existing character, have created buildings which have enhanced the look of the village. Warnham is lucky in that it has good rail and road connections but no traffic problem, the main London to Horsham road skirting the eastern edge of the village. It also has a thriving local industry, the works which produce many of the famous Horsham bricks being situated alongside the railway line.

Warnham's most famous son is Percy Shelley, although it has to be said that the poet can have had few fond memories of his home. This was Field Place, a large house south-west of the village, dating chiefly from the late seventeenth and middle eighteenth centuries. The family was already long established in Sussex and both Percy's, father and grandfather, felt that writing poetry was no way of maintaining its position. Indeed the father was so aggrieved by his son's lack of interest in leading the sort of life befitting the heir to a country estate that he banned him from the house. He returned on the death of his grandfather in 1815 but was not even allowed to hear the will, and thus practically all of Shelley's mature work was done away from Sussex. There is no memorial to the poet in Warnham church although the deaths of two of his sisters and his eleven-year-old son Charles are recorded on a family tablet on the south wall.

Of far greater account within Warnham was Michael Turner who was born in 1796 and died in 1885. He was leader of the choir and the relics of his office are preserved in a glass case inside the church. These consist of a viol, a tuning-fork and some music books, along with his photograph. He obviously took great pride in his appearance, as well he might, for he was also parish clerk and sexton for fifty years and as such was regarded as "headsman of the village". By trade he was a shoemaker; all these activities seem to have kept him so busy that although much sought after he never got around to marriage.

St Margaret's Church, Warnham, was heavily restored in Victorian times by Sir Arthur Blomfield, who also built the village school and did a good deal of work on Warnham Court, a large house immediately to the south of the village; one of his rather jolly, ornate lodges sits beside some of the newest houses in Warnham, homes which are a good deal more traditional with their local red brick and tiles.

Rusper and Warnham are close enough to Horsham for its pull on them to be considerable. It used to be said that Horsham and Chichester were the only real towns in West Sussex. This is no longer true, but as Billingshurst, Pulborough, Midhurst, Petworth, Selsey, Henfield, Storrington, Steyning, Burgess Hill, Hassocks, Crawley and East Grinstead have all grown into towns so Horsham has kept pace and grown too. In the last few years the rate of its expansion has been almost as dramatic as that of Crawley, and although the oldest part immediately south of the Carfax is untouched, the rest, particularly to the north of the Carfax, has been transformed. The former village of Roffey on the Crawley road is now a suburb as is Broadbridge Heath where the A281 Guildford and the A264 Bognor roads diverge.

Slinfold, situated between the A281 and the A29, is perhaps the best kept village in all Sussex. Nothing is out of place, there are no unnecessary signs of wires, the paintwork of the houses and cottages is spotless, the gardens are immaculate and in the churchyard each variety of rose is carefully labelled. Confirmation of the strong sense of community in Slinfold is the list of clubs, societies and other organizations displayed on the village notice board. It totals twenty and is worth giving in full for it reveals with some precision the interests and aspirations not only of the people of Slinfold but of many other similar Sussex villages. Here it is— Royal British Legion, Mother's Union, Women's Institute, Young Wives, Music Circle, Conservative Association, Slinfold Amenity Society, Horticultural Society, Bellringers, Cumming Memorial Club (Social Club), Cricket Club, Football Club, Lawn Tennis Club, Parish Council, Parochial Church Council, Prescription Service, School Management Committee, Scouts, Slinfold Singers, Thursday Club (Senior Citizens).

The next station from Slinfold along the disused branch line which once ran from Horsham to Guildford was Rudgwick. It was the last before it crossed into Surrey and the parish church of Holy Trinity stands within a few yards of the border. A block of shops has been built on the site of the station down at the bottom end of the village on the main street which forms part of the B2128 to Cranleigh and Guildford. As at Warnham there has been a good deal of building this century. The oldest part of the village is the north end, dominated by the church of Holy Trinity which is unusual in that it is chiefly early fourteenth century, a period which saw little church building in Sussex. Holy Trinity stands on rising ground; if one should slip one might suffer the not alto- gether unpleasant sensation of tumbling into the bar of the Queen's Head which marks the western boundary of the church- yard. The Queen's Head is perhaps the most handsome building in Rudgwick, a lovely mixture of stone, brick, weather-boarding and tiles; opposite is the village hall erected "In commemoration of Queen Victoria's Long Reign, 1837–97".

Beyond Rudgwick and its satellite of Bucks Green astride the A281 we move into an area where the railway never ventured and where there are no main roads. The lingering vestiges of suburbia extend no further than Bucks Green and London might be one hundred rather than thirty miles away. The unclassified road from Rudgwick follows a devious route and eventually comes to Lox- wood. In the centre of the village is an attractive duckpond and beside it a row of shops, or rather a small department store which includes a garage. Until recently this belonged to a religious sect known as the Cokelers.

Officially called the Society of Dependents, they have been known as Cokelers ever since their inaugural meeting at Loxwood in 1850 when they drank cocoa specially brought down from London, much to the amazement of the locals. The principal attributes of the sect were thrift, abstinence, a good business sense and a devotion to worship, although they sound rather dull for they disapproved of dancing, singing, cut flowers, bank holidays, and, most surprisingly, marriage. They didn't actually forbid it, which was just as well or there would soon have been no Cokelers left, but any couple wishing to marry had to do so in the parish church.

Their founder was a London shoemaker, John Sirgood, and so effective a preacher was he that in 1861 the local vicar and churchwardens threatened him with legal action if he continued with his "unlawful meetings". In the event the Cokelers were let be and when Sirgood died in 1885 he had a following of almost 2,000. Over the years communities were set up in a number of Sussex villages, including Northchapel, Warnham, Kirdford and Felpham, and in Hove and Chichester. The lives of the Cokelers were centred on their chapels and their stores and as these thrifty people invested their savings in these latter their prosperity grew. In 1931 there were thirteen salesmen and assistants at Northchapel and no less than thirty-one at Warnham, whilst at the main store at Loxwood almost any commodity imaginable, including a motor car, could be obtained. The assistants there continued to wear Victorian costume until after World War II. The sect still exists and I met an elderly lady member in Loxwood; in the words of Earl Winterton, writing in the *Sussex County Magazine* in 1931, "Should the Sect ever die out . . . Sussex will be the poorer for the loss of a kindly and honest set of people".

Kirdford, Plaistow, Ifold and Durfold Wood form one parish of 12,500 acres, the largest in West Sussex. Only Kirdford and

Plaistow can really claim to be villages, the parish church being at Kirdford with a chapel-of-ease at Plaistow. The area attracts few visitors for it is far from the sea and bisected by no through routes. It had its period of importance from the thirteenth to the sixteenth centuries when the glass-making industry flourished. This was centred on Chiddingfold, across the border in Surrey, but it was carried on throughout the district extending as far south as Kirdford. A few fragments of local glass in the church windows and names such as Glasshouse Lane and Glasshouse Copse are about all that remain. The only industry of any significance to be found today is a large fruit-growing co-operative at Kirdford, which provides many of the local people with employment. Close to it is an estate known as Townfield, but the name is somewhat fanciful for Kirdford could never have been anything grander than a not very large village. Only when there is a skittles match at the pub opposite the church is there any great stir of activity. The nearest shopping centres are Petworth to the south and Billingshurst to the east, both about five miles away.

Plaistow occupies the northern part of the parish, with a Victorian church, Holy Trinity, built on the site of a medieval timber-framed one. Beside this is the school which bears the following inscription:

> John Napper Esq. of Ifold. Having more than 30 years filled the office of chairman of the Guardians of the Petworth Union, a fund was raised for the purpose of presenting to him a testimonial. The fund largely augmented by him he generously donated to the erection of this building, AD 1869.

The union was, of course, the workhouse. Today we should not perhaps think that to be chairman of such a concern was anything to commemorate, but it was all that stood between the poor of the parish and starvation and death. A benevolent chairman, as it would seem John Napper was, could make life in the workhouse quite tolerable and he might well personally contribute towards its upkeep.

Plaistow Place is a fine sixteenth-century half-timbered house near the village; on the green is a stunted tree standing on a knoll which is said to have been planted by Nell Gwyn when she was staying at the house on account of having fallen out of favour with King Charles. One wonders how she occupied herself during her banishment for one who loved London and the court must have found time hung heavily in quiet Plaistow. The green is very fine with few buildings around it and with some magnificent oak trees in its centre. It stands slightly above the village and from it one may look across the Weald, past Petworth to the South Downs. Although trees block the view, Blackdown, the highest point in Sussex, lies a good deal nearer, to the east. An excellent view of its 918 feet high summit is to be obtained from Ebernoe, originally part of the parish of Kirdford, and Plaistow but transferred in 1927 to Northchapel, the next village to the east.

Ebernoe has been called "the most remote village in Sussex". 'Remote' in this context is a relative term and would be understood to mean something a good deal further from civilization in the west of Scotland or Ireland, for example; one might also question whether there is enough of Ebernoe to call itself a village at all. However, *The Times* so defined it on 11 April 1938, so we may allow ourselves to do so too. The occasion was the beginning of British Summer Time and *The Times* recorded that Ebernoe paid it scant regard. In order to comply with the law the sexton put the church clock on an hour, and the cows were milked half an hour earlier to oblige the customers, but for the rest the 200 inhabitants carried on as before, left their clocks and watches unaltered and slept on for an extra hour.

Ebernoe, as one approaches it from Kirdford, apparently consists of little more than a public telephone box beside a narrow lane deep in the woods. If one looks closely one can see some distance back on the north side of the lane Ebernoe House, dating from the late eighteenth century, whilst on the opposite side is a grass track leading through the trees to a clearing in which stands the church and the school house. The latter is now a private residence but the former, built in 1868, is still in regular use. To mark its centenary a history of the parish was compiled and this is displayed inside the church. Further evidence of the continuing care of this small and scattered community for its church is the altar carpet which was woven by parishioners in 1960; in the pattern are depicted the wild flowers which surround the church. The latest adornment is a collage telling the history of Ebernoe which was made by thirty-seven eleven-year-old children from the Central Church of England School in Chichester after they had spent a week on environmental studies at Ebernoe. The collage was presented to Ebernoe in 1973. Ebernoe people have little need of the outside world and until twenty years ago there was no electricity or piped water in the village. They were, and in many ways still are, self-sufficient, brewing their own beer and keeping bees and a few cows, pigs and goats each. Once a year the outside world discovers Ebernoe when Puck Fair comes round, On St James's Day at the end of July a horned sheep is roasted whole on the cricket ground, a match takes place between Ebernoe and the neighbouring village of Lurgashall, and at the end of the day the horns of the sheep are given to the highest scorer. The carcase takes four to five hours to roast and some 5 cwt. of oak cord-wood are needed for the fire. Coconut shies and various other sideshows accompany the match. The fair is said to go back 500 years, and until the eighteenth century it was a fair at which horns, used in the manufacture of cups, spoons, forks, etc., were sold. Until World War I gypsies attended the fair in great numbers; in the 1920s and 1930s it was in decline but the late 1930s saw a revival and after World War II it flourished again. The fair over, Ebernoe goes back to sleep for another year, its site once again an empty field overlooked by a solitary house. The lane which is Ebernoe's only access to the outside bisects the fair field; one may stand in its centre if not for hours then for many minutes, without fear of disturbance.

Although well hidden from it, Ebernoe is not so very far from the main A283 Guildford to Chichester road. Ebernoe's nearest shops are at Northchapel, the last village on the road on the

Sussex side of the border. Originally its church was a chapel-at-ease belonging to the parish of Petworth; Northchapel became a parish in its own right in 1716. Four miles east of Northchapel is Fernhurst, and in many ways the villages are twins. They are of about the same size, each lies on a main road linking Guildford and Chichester, and between them and dominating both is Blackdown. Blackdown Hill gets its name both from the colour of the earth on its western slopes and from the dark heather and firs which cover it and in the evening when the sun is setting behind it, it looks black indeed. It only just qualifies as a Sussex hill for it belongs to the Haslemere range; its northern slopes are in Surrey and it has a good deal of the feeling of that county about it. Tennyson had a summer home, Aldworth House, built for himself on the eastern side of the hill, the foundation stone being laid on 23rd April 1869, Shakespeare's birthday; the lane which leads to it from Haslemere is called Tennyson's Lane. The National Trust owns 602 acres of Blackdown, the greatest part of it being donated by Mr E. W. Hunter in 1944 in memory of his wife. Tennyson looked out from his house and wrote:

> You came and looked, and loved the view,
> Long known and loved by me,
> Green Sussex fading into blue
> With one gray glimpse of sea.

The one glimpse is said to be of Pevensey Bay, some fifty miles away. From hereabouts it is possible to travel in a straight line for seventy miles to Rye at the other end of the county. The Vicar of Fernhurst, down beneath Blackdown, told me that the people of Rye claim that there are no less than seven cathedrals nearer to them than their own one at Chichester, the seven being Canterbury, Rochester, St Paul's and Westminster Abbey, and Abbeville, Amiens and Lille in France. He rather resented the fact that although he had spent all his life in Sussex parishes he now had to put as his address Fernhurst Vicarage, Haslemere, Surrey. He confessed that there were many worse places to owe allegiance to and indeed the towns and villages around Blackdown, both in Surrey and Sussex, stand securely rooted in a fertile and richly wooded landscape and exude an air of well-ordered, long-experienced, quiet prosperity. I talked to the vicar when Fernhurst looked at its very best on a warm evening in early summer. The organist and the bellringers were practising for the crowning of the May Queen next day and across the green an ancient but immaculate tractor with bright orange wheels was pulling a mower across the field upon which the celebrations were to take place under Blackdown.

Fernhurst and Northchapel are full of fine old houses, each has an old church—Fernhurst's originally twelfth century, North-chapel's fourteenth, both heavily restored in the nineteenth century —but neither village is remote or sleepy. There are a number of modern houses in each, Haslemere and Midhurst are within easy reach, and the Plant Protection Division of ICI has an extensive research establishment at Verdley on the road from Fernhurst to Northchapel which employs 500 local people and is visited by scientists and horticulturalists from all over the world. There was once a castle at Verdley; it gradually fell into decay, assisted by the local people who re-employed its stones for road-building, and even its foundations were dug out in 1880 to pave the rides through Verdley Wood. Now its site has disappeared, grown over by Douglas firs and thorn bushes.

In this western area of Sussex, close to Surrey and Hampshire, cricket first became a national sport. One of the greatest of the early cricketers, Noah Mann, was an innkeeper and cobbler at Northchapel. He played for the most famous club of all, Hambledon in Surrey, and would ride his horse to and from matches there. He died at the early age of thirty-three. Fernhurst has its own history, *The Story of a Sussex Village*, written by Alice M. Tudor and published in Guildford in 1934. One of the most interesting statistics it records is that 250 members of the Luff family were baptized in the church between 1547 and 1847. Luffs can still be found in the district, one of them being the local funeral director.

The summit of Blackdown actually lies within the parish of Lurgashall. The village, much smaller than either Fernhurst or Northchapel, is between and to the south of them. Approached by narrow, twisting lanes, it is nearly all green, its chief glory being the parish church of St Lawrence. The church is situated at the north-east corner of the green, amongst trees, which inevitably make its interior rather dark, and which is accentuated by the absence of windows in the south wall of the nave. In some churches this lack of light would be depressing, but here where there is little distracting decoration it works to its advantage, creating an atmosphere of calm and peace. There is one attractive modern stained glass window in memory of a young man of the parish who died in 1952 at the age of twenty-seven and a beautiful older one, all green and yellow, at the west end of the church. St Lawrence's possesses what is claimed to be a feature unique in England, an early seventeenth-century wooden porch which extends the length of the south wall. It was enclosed in 1622 in order that it might be used as the village school. In the choir is another interesting wooden object, a chest with the inscription "Thomas Albrey and James Osborn, churchwardens, 1667" roughly carved on it.

South of Lurgashall is the hamlet of Lickfold, which has some quaint cottages, and beyond this, almost on the A272 Winchester to Heathfield road but out of sight of it, is Lodsworth. Its setting on the side of a valley is superb and it is a beautiful, quite large and very well kept village. The brief guide to the parish church begins with the words "Whatever the world may say, we love our church and hope you will find something here to please you." It has been stated elsewhere that the church has virtually no architectural merit. The author of the guide was clearly aware of this and one sympathizes with the sadness implicit in the phrasing he has chosen. One cannot simply treat a church as an aesthetic exercise; even on that level St Peter's, Lodsworth— Victorian restoration notwithstanding—is not without its merits. I have seldom seen a church upon which more care has been lavished. The side chapel was dedicated in 1968 to the local children, the kneelers are beautifully embroidered with various motifs, there is a simple altar made of Northumbrian stone and a new porch has been carefully and skilfully added containing a richly coloured stained glass window depicting St Nicholas. A lady arranging flowers took considerable pleasure in conducting me round the chapel, although she regretted that with so many retired people living at Lodsworth there were no longer enough local children for the school to be kept open and they now went on the bus to Midhurst. Lodsworth had a famous chess club, founded by the vicar, the Rev. C. S. Chilver, in 1889; in 1920 it was the best in all Sussex, and at its fiftieth anniversary some of the original members were still playing. Incidentally, the church, rather than dominating the village as in so many Sussex villages, is difficult to find. It lies quite near the centre down a steep, narrow lane amongst trees and cannot be seen from the main road.

Tillington is another handsome village, situated to the southeast of Lodsworth against the south-west corner of the grounds of Petworth Place, a closely grouped collection of mainly stone buildings extending down the hill from the church to the Petworth to Midhurst road. Inside the church, past the studded, leather-covered doors, are many memorials, including some to the Mitford family who were prominent locally. Two in particular catch the eye. The first dates from 1909 and was put up in thankfulness for the recovery from a serious accident of the eleven-year-old William Mitford. Beside it, fifty-five years on, is one to the memory of the same William who in the fullness of time became church-warden and served for twenty years.

The next village along the A272 is Easebourne. If one is not looking for it one might miss it, for Easebourne is close enough to Midhurst to be mistaken for part of that town. But it is a true village with its own church and shops clustered around the main road. Easebourne comes to an abrupt end at the east wall of the churchyard. Beyond are the spacious, undulating grounds of Cowdray Park, populated by groves of tall beeches, oaks, chestnuts and polo players. The polo ground is probably the most famous in the country; the Duke of Edinburgh and Prince Charles often play there, watched by the Queen. Down the slope of the park below Easebourne are the dramatic ruins of the Elizabethan Cowdray House. The house was abandoned after a fire in 1793 and a replacement erected a mile to the east.

The parishioners of Easebourne at one time shared their church with some Benedictine nuns from an adjoining priory. They were dispersed by Henry VIII and practically nothing of that part of the church used by the nuns remains. The priory itself survives, converted into the vicarage. There was a sad air about Easebourne when I last visited it; the churchwardens had had to complete the latest edition of the parish magazine, for the vicar—a man in early middle age—had died suddenly and unexpectedly, and the sense of loss felt in the parish was apparent.

With Easebourne, standing astride the road linking the cathedral cities of Winchester and Canterbury, we reach the end of this chapter. Midhurst, a few hundred yards away, is the most northwesterly town in the county; beyond it is still border country, but now it is Hampshire rather than Surrey which lies on the other side.

# 3

## *Along the Hampshire Border*

THE area bounded by the Hampshire border, the Petersfield–Petworth road, the Petworth–Chichester one and the Downs has a remote, untouched air, its relatively few inhabitants being concerned chiefly with farming; visitors are few, tea houses are fewer. South Harting is the only really large village and the lanes, except in high summer, are generally muddy. It is no wonder that the branch lines which ran through it closed long ago, whilst buses are a rather less familiar sight than horses, or so it seems.

Petersfield, although in Hampshire, is the focal point of the area. It is nearly four times as large as Midhurst, ten miles to the east, and has a railway station on the Waterloo to Portsmouth main line.

South Harting makes the most of its setting under the Downs, which this far west are extensively wooded, and is full of handsome brick, clunch (soft white limestone) and some tile-hung and stone cottages and houses. The parish church, with the unusual and attractive name of St Mary and St Gabriel, is as good a piece of architecture as any in the Hartings, and dates principally from the fourteenth century. The interior is full of interest, with a lovely and elaborate Elizabethan wooden roof to the chancel, replacing one burnt in a serious fire around 1576, some show cases at the back which form a small museum containing items ranging from relics of Torbury hillfort of 500 B.C. to a clarinet used to accompany singing in the church before the organ was installed in 1855, and some rather grand tombs. Externally the most striking feature of St Mary and St Gabriel's is its pale green copper spire; it is seen to its best advantage from the top of the hill where the Petersfield road climbs out of the village, when the sun shines upon it, standing out against the deep green of the wooded downs beyond. The spire was virtually wrecked during a gale in September 1935 but an appeal for £500 succeeded and it was restored.

A number of famous people have lived in and around Harting, including Anthony Trollope, Lady Hamilton, H. G. Wells and George Romney, a mixed bunch indeed. Trollope lived at Harting Grange from 1880 to his death in 1882—although he actually died in London—and wrote four books and one unfinished one there. Amongst his visitors was Millais, whilst in an earlier age another painter, Romney, came to Uppark, a lovely seventeenth-century house in a superb setting up on the Downs just south of Harting. The object of Romney's visit was one Emily Lyon, an unusually attractive girl in her late teens, living at Uppark in the 'care' of Sir Harry Fetherstonhaugh its owner. Sir Harry was a great one for entertaining and some of the most notable people of the day came to the house, including the Prince Regent. Another guest was Sir William Hamilton, whom Emily married, thus becoming Lady Hamilton, and, later, Nelson's Emma. H. G. Wells also lived at Uppark, albeit in a much more humble style, for his mother was housekeeper there. His parents had met at the house, his father being gardener, and when they married they set up shop in Bromley, where H. G. was born. However, the business failed and Wells's mother came back to Uppark, her son working for two years as a chemist's assistant in a shop in Midhurst. He later used his experiences there in *Kipps*, and Uppark features as Bladesover in *Tono-Bungay*. Earlier in the century the house had been offered to the Duke of Wellington by the nation but he declined it on account of the steepness of the hill leading to it from Harting. This historic house may be visited by the public for it was handed over to the National Trust by Admiral Sir Herbert Meade-Fetherston-haugh in 1954.

Lying north-east of the Hartings, on the Petersfield–Midhurst road, are Rogate and Trotton. It is still very much border country; one of the local papers is the *Portsmouth News* and the correct postal address of Rogate is Rogate, Petersfield, Hants. Trotton has a lovely five-arched bridge over the Rother, dating back to the early fifteenth century, and in the parish church of St George there are some notable relics, one of them being a wall painting of the Last Judgement, said to date from around 1380. Two brasses, belonging to the Camoys family, are of exceptional interest. The memorial to Margaret, Lady Camoys dates from 1310 and is thus the oldest known brass to a woman in the country, whilst that of 1419 to Thomas, Lord Camoys and his wife is one of the largest and most magnificent. It was this Lord Camoys who was responsible for the building of Trotton Bridge. He fought at Agincourt; his wife had previously been married to Hotspur and is Kate of *The Taming of the Shrew*. It may well be that other Trotton men were at Agincourt for the village was famous for its archers and it has been suggested that the grooves on the door jambs at the west end of the church were worn by the generations sharpening their arrows. For centuries a law existed in England that all youths and men should practise archery on Sunday afternoons and feast days, and whilst this often took place in a field known as the butts, it was just as common for the churchyard to be used.

Rogate was a great iron-working area in the sixteenth and seventeenth centuries and also supplied wood for ship-building. Today wood still plays an important part in the village's economy, there being a thriving industry producing split chestnut palings. Until a little while ago there was a toy factory, which employed local people, in the old water mill at Durford, to the west of the village and close to the site of Durford Abbey, an Augustinian establishment dissolved by Henry VIII. Other Durford people work as far away as London and Portsmouth, travelling on the train from Petersfield, and the village has long associations with the Navy. There are two pubs but only one shop in the village, a large Gothic Revival house immediately to the south belonging to King's College,

London, and some quite beautiful old people's homes beside the church. These were built by the Rogate and Terwick Housing Association in 1970, constructed of red brick and white-painted weather-boarding, with lots of windows which look out across the churchyard and the carefully tended gardens. They are an example of all that is best in modern architecture, restrained but with plenty of interesting angles so that there is no sense of monotony, very well lit but still allowing as much privacy as the occupants care to have and perfectly integrated with the existing buildings and setting. The guide to the parish church is particularly comprehensive and gives some nice glimpses of village life. The designer of the war memorial cross, Sir Ninian Comper, wrote to the Vicar that he liked it "best of the many I have designed: partly because I heard that the gypsies like it". In the nineteenth century many of the vicars, as elsewhere in the county, were hardly ever seen in the village. The school was opened in January 1868 and the original buildings, much modernized, are still in use; the five-thousandth child was enrolled in April 1974.

The far north-west corner of the county has something of the air of no-man's-land about it, not quite Hampshire but not truly Sussex, or so it seems to the outsider. It is heavily wooded and dominated by the northern ridge along which the London to Portsmouth road and railway line run and which culminates in the 919 feet high Blackdown to the east and the 888 feet high Butser Hill to the west. Most of this ridge is in Hampshire and two villages on the Portsmouth road immediately north of Petersfield, Hill Brow and Rake, are divided between Sussex and Hampshire. Charcoal burning continued in this area until recently, around the hamlets of Milland and Milland Marsh, and chestnut fencing is still made here. In autumn the surfaces of the lanes and by-roads are in places practically invisible under a thick carpet of chestnuts.

Linchmere is the most north-westerly village in Sussex, 500 feet above sea level, equidistant from Liphook and Haslemere barely two miles distant, but nevertheless remote and as quiet a spot as any in the county. The Rev. A. A. Evans feared for its future in the 1920s, complaining that builders were at work "not in response to a genuine need, but as a commercial speculation", but his apprehensions were unfounded for the village has long since absorbed the newcomers. Twentieth-century builders have also left their mark on the parish church of St Peter, but in a sensitive and sympathetic manner. They have merely added to an established pattern for there have been many rebuildings over the centuries and although little of the original Norman work remains St Peter's is a handsome church, both inside and out. Its guidebook claims, with some justification, that the view across the Weald from its position 500 feet up "is one of the finest in Sussex". It can best be appreciated from a seat by the south wall given by a former vicar and his wife, Harold and Marjorie Dyer, to mark "ten happy years in Linchmere". On the north wall of the churchyard are a number of memorials to local people, including "Maria Teresa Shephard, a fellow of the Institute of Landscape Gardeners and maker of gardens in Britain and Italy" and Richard Dimbleby.

The history of the churches of Treyford, Elsted and Didling, east of the Hartings, is fascinating and complex. In the mid-nineteenth century the Rector of the three parishes appealed to Mrs Vernon Harcourt of West Dean House who owned most of the land thereabouts for money to restore Elsted and Treyford churches. Her answer was that she would erect a great new one between the two. The Rector objected that the parishioners of both would have to walk further but was informed by Mrs Harcourt that "If they really want to worship they will come". Time, the parishioners, and possibly Providence proved her wrong, for the great church of St Peter's she had erected and which came to be known as the "Cathedral of the Downs" was never popular and within 100 years showed signs of severe structural failure. The original Treyford church was by then in ruins and St Paul's, Elsted, in a very sad state, although still in use. The Rector of Elsted set up a world-wide appeal fund for the restoration of St Paul's and in November 1951 the tiny but beautiful little church was rededicated by Bishop Bell of Chichester.

At the same time the "Cathedral of the Downs" was completely demolished with the aid of explosives.

Elsted is an attractive, fairly compact flint village approached from the north through an archway of trees; Treyford is smaller and much more scattered as is Didling (which takes its name from a Saxon chief Dyddel who settled here) with but eleven houses and some thirty parishioners. Its church has also been restored fairly recently. It stands at the end of a very muddy lane all on its own under the Downs, small but full of history. Known as the Shepherds' Church, although there are less sheep about here than there used to be, it is constructed of stone imported from the Isle of Wight and from Caen, as well as of brick and local flint. It once had a ghost which took the form of a "high pitched soprano, almost like falsetto, but very pure and in tune with the hymn", heard by many of the congregation and the organist on a number of occasions.

Just how small and closely knit a Sussex village community can be may be gauged from the parish notes of Elsted and Treford-cum-Didling. They record that in September 1975 five new children joined the village school, "making a total of 38 in all", the smallest member of the infant class being a kitten belonging to Philip and Richard Young. Further on there is an appeal for volunteers to drive the Elsted members home from the Darby and Joan Club at Harting on Tuesday afternoons, a note that Downview Cottage has been bought by a couple from Haslemere, that Malcolm Hill hopes to be back working on the farm fairly soon after a tractor accident, and finally some reminiscences by an elderly inhabitant of Didling recalling an Italian who worked on a local farm sixty years ago and pushed a barrel-organ to Midhurst and the surrounding villages, and a German brass band which came from Harting, accompanied by a bear on a chain.

Cocking is rather more worldly, being situated on the main Haslemere to Chichester road, and is a handsome village. Much of it is owned by the Cowdray estate and therefore the deep yellow paintwork sported by estates property and which is such

Modern Horsham brick and tile-hung cottages at Warnham

The village stores, Slinfold

Loxwood

Fernhurst on a May evening

(*above*) Easebourne. (*below*) South Harting, with the copper-covered spire of St Mary and St Gabriel prominent. (*overleaf*) West Itchenor, looking across the harbour towards Bosham

The old people's homes at Rogate

Flintstone at West Marden

East Wittering

West Wittering

Pagham beach in December

Climping beach in June

a feature of the villages around Midhurst is much in evidence. Cocking once belonged to Edward the Confessor, and passed into the Montague family in Elizabethan times thus becoming part of the Cowdray estate. Cocking church is in a gorgeous setting, standing on a hillock with a stream at the bottom and beyond this the steep rise of the Downs. There are a great many iron tombstones in the churchyard, the only date I could decipher being 1899, which puts it well beyond the last Sussex forged iron, but it may be that the others were older, certainly thay had stood long enough to prove that inscriptions in iron are not as durable as those in stone. In the main street there is an inn called the Richard Cobden, recalling that the great free-trader bought a house at nearby Heyshott out of the £80,000 given him by a grateful nation and is buried at West Lavington, a couple of miles up the road from Cocking. Cardinal Manning, before his conversion to the Roman faith, lived at Lavington House and preached his last sermon as a priest of the Church of England at the parish church of St Peter's, East Lavington, in 1851.

Selham, south of the Midhurst to Petworth road, is a tiny place but worth a visit if only to see the windows in the church around which is woven a fascinating story. Two of them ask the parishioners to pray for various exalted rulers of medieval times, a request which puzzled a good many people for a number of years; the explanation emerged only very recently. An old lady died in London in 1970 and left £500, two christening mugs and a leatherbound book to Selham. The book revealed that she was the last surviving descendant of the Rev. Blackburn who had been rector of Selham for over fifty years in the nineteenth century. His family had made their money in trade, not quite 'the thing' in Victorian times, but he had married a Miss Clutterbuck who apparently had a fairly genuine claim to be descended from the Plantagenets, and this so tickled the Rev. Blackburn that he had the stained-glass windows in question installed, "the arms of my children's ancestors", as he once remarked.

Immediately south of Cocking the main road cuts through the

D

Downs and there, set on a hillside at Singleton, is the most modern
and at the same time one of the oldest villages in Sussex. Actually
there are two villages at Singleton. The original one, in the valley
through which the main road runs, called Silletone in Domesday,
is still inhabited and flourishing, although its period of fame, or
notoriety, lasted for less than a century and has long since gone.
This was after Goodwood race-course was opened in 1801 up on
the Downs above the village. Visitors to the races stayed in Singleton and some of them made a great racket about the place, bringing
down upon their heads the wrath of the Rector and the attentions
of the Chief Constable. A handsome station was built when the
railway arrived in 1880 with a carpet and a stained-glass window
in the waiting room to impress the Duke of Richmond and Willie
James, friend of the Prince of Wales. The Prince kept his horses
at Singleton. The coming of the motor car meant people had no
longer to stay in the neighbourhood and when the Season got under
way again in 1919 Society passed Singleton by.

Some fifty years later Singleton stepped back into the limelight
when it was decided to establish a second village in the form of an
open-air museum on land donated by the Edward James Foundation.

The Museum opened in May 1971 and as I write it consists of
nineteen exhibits. Many of these are buildings, removed from their
original sites—some within, some without the county—when
threatened with demolition and re-erected at Singleton. What is
especially striking, and instructive, about each re-erection is that
we are able to experience something of what it was like to live in
when it was new. This means that when we walk into the timber-
frame house which was brought from Bough Beech, near Tonbridge,
Kent, and probably goes back to the late fourteenth century, our
eyes immediately begin to smart because there is no chimney, only
a vent in the gable, to let the smoke escape from the fire burning
in the middle of the floor. The house is divided into two bays with
one upstairs room; there is no glass in the windows, and there
would have been very little furniture, perhaps not even a bed but

merely blankets or rugs laid out on the floor. This house and others at Singleton graphically illustrate how considerable has been the alteration and modernization to enable any old house or cottage built before the nineteenth century—or even, in the case of many cottages, the present century to remain habitable today. As well as the buildings there are exhibits illustrating ancient crafts, such as pottery, woodcrafts and charcoal burning. The Museum is run chiefly by volunteers with a very small paid staff and depends on admission money and subscriptions to continue its work. It lays great emphasis on its primary aim which is to preserve buildings in their original sites, and only moves them to Singleton as a last resort. However, it is gradually building up a representative collection of houses, cottages, barns, public buildings, etc. which already forms one of the most fascinating villages in the county.

West Dean up the hill from Singleton is an idyllic place, reached by narrow lanes leading down from the A286 to a wooded valley, the stone houses and cottages dotted amongst trees, and luxuriant hedgerows. In the churchyard on the hillside are numerous graves to the Boxalls, a prolific local family. In 1936 James and Caroline Boxall celebrated their diamond wedding anniversary; they were the parents of no less than twenty-seven children, including one set of triplets and two pairs of twins, their oldest child was fifty-nine years old and they had a great many grandchildren and great-grandchildren. James had lived all his life in West Dean, Caroline came from Singleton. Contemporary with them were Mr and Mrs Willie James, who lived in West Dean House on the eastern side of the village. They were great friends of King Edward VII and he often stayed with them. Mrs James was a talented amateur actress and in the year the King died she played the lead in a charity matinée in aid of Queen Alexandra's nurses at the Brighton Palladium during the King's last visit to Brighton. Their house is now an arts centre. Next to it is the church, a plain, pleasant building, rebuilt in the 1930s after a bad fire.

South again along the A283 and the last village before Chichester is Lavant which is really three villages in one, East, West, and Mid.

The civil parishes were combined in 1872, the ecclesiastical ones eight years later, although there are still two churches, St Nicholas in Mid Lavant—which is on the main road beside the old railway station—and the parish church of St Mary's up the hill in East Lavant. Mid Lavant suffers from a traffic problem for the road through the village is rather narrow and there is a proposal before the Parish Council as I write to set back the wall around the churchyard to improve matters. In the same edition of the *Lavant News* where I learnt this I also came across a complaint which in essence goes echoing back through the ages to the beginnings of village life. The village green belongs to everyone, but the people of Lavant found, as no doubt every preceding generation had, that not all the activities to which it is put are compatible. The particular complaint concerned youngsters playing golf which, it was alleged, "interfered with the comfort of other users of the Green, cut up the turf and resulted in balls very nearly smashing through windows". A parent argued that it was the only safe place for the boys to play and in the end the eminently sensible solution arrived at was that "no action should be taken providing no annoyance was caused to other people and that the divots were trodden back in".

A by-road leads westwards from Lavant under the Downs through the hamlet of West Stoke with its tiny church standing beside a handsome eighteenth-century house to the Ashlings, Funtingdon, Hambrook and Woodmancote. East and West Ashling are sizeable hamlets, as are Woodmancote and Hambrook; only Funtingdon is really a village. There are some big houses as well as the usual flint and brick cottages in Funtingdon, and a lovely, very long, low thatched house which is now a restaurant. The heavily restored church of St Mary's stands at the east end of the village, with fields on two sides. Amongst the tombs in the churchyard is that of Sir Proud William Parry Wallis, CCB, Admiral of the Fleet who died in 1892 at the age of 100.

Up in the Downs north of Funtingdon, on the road to the Hartings, are the Mardens, North, Up, East and West. West Marden, although it is the only one without a church, is the biggest. For all that it is hardly more than a hamlet, set in gently rolling, wooded countryside. Stoughton and Walderton, immediately south of the Hartings, are similarly either large hamlets or small villages, depending upon one's interpretation of each definition. Walderton has no church but Stoughton has an eleventh-century one which is virtually original with little subsequent addition or restoration.

Compton is the most northerly and the largest of the group of woodland communities set amongst the valleys of the southern slopes of the Downs between Chichester and the Hampshire border. Despite its relative size it shares the quiet, undisturbed air common to them all. It is, however, near enough to Portsmouth to have attracted seafarers long before the motor car made the journey a matter of minutes rather than hours and in the church are three brass plaques of identical design to three Admiral Hornbys. The first started his career in Nelson's time, the last served in the First World War and died at the age of ninety in 1956. The Hornbys were Lords of the Manor in Victorian times and Admiral Sir Phipps Hornby was chairman of the committee which presided over the restoration of the church. He ensured that three rows of pews were reserved for his household.

If we take the B2146 from Compton back to West Marden and then head westwards up the hill to the appropriately named hamlet of Forestside, we can then run parallel to the Hampshire border through woodlands, past the entrance to Stansted House, and so come down to sea level and a dramatically different landscape. Westbourne is, as one might suppose, as far west as one can go in Sussex; it is a true village but it is also suburbia, part of that enormous conglomeration which has grown up behind Portsmouth and which now extends to beyond Southampton. All that apparently separates it from Havant in Hampshire is a West Sussex sign by the roadside, but if one explores Westbourne one finds a good deal of village atmosphere. The church of St John the Baptist is mostly of the twelfth and thirteenth centuries with a small round-headed window in the east wall of the belfry which was opened out in 1963 and which suggests that the oldest part of the church is Saxon. Outside is an avenue of yew trees planted in 1545 which, it is claimed, "is probably the oldest and finest in England". It is certainly very handsome, although there are individual trees elsewhere in Sussex, let alone beyond the borders of the county, which are a great deal older. The spire, which dates from the latter part of the eighteenth century, was a gift from the Lord of the Manor, the Earl of Halifax. He offered the parishioners either this or an endowment for a Sunday afternoon sermon; they chose the former "because it would point to heaven whereas a sermon might not". In addition to its church and churchyard Westbourne possesses some attractive, winding streets, lined with Victorian and earlier buildings, which certainly dispel the initial impression of twentieth-century suburbia.

The same cannot be said of Southbourne, across the river from the Hampshire town of Emsworth. This really is pure suburbia, with its late Victorian red-brick church, and its semi-detacheds strung out along the A27 coast road. It is not without a certain village atmosphere, and it has links with other Sussex villages, but in spirit it belongs to the Portsmouth and Havant suburbs. The same is largely true of Nutbourne to the east, but due south is West Thorney which belongs to a quite different category. As late as the 1930s it was described in the *Sussex County Magazine* as "Possibly the most isolated and unspoiled area in Sussex". The reader may have come across similar descriptions applied to other parts of the county, but certainly it was an out-of-the-way spot. Then in 1934 an aerodrome was proposed on Thorney Island and although nothing was done for a year or so it was eventually built and remained RAF property until the summer of 1976 when it was handed over to the Navy. The road to the church and the village passes right through the aerodrome and although the public had access in RAF days the airman guarding the gate did not always grant it with very good grace. Some old cottages remain, as does the twelfth-thirteenth-century church by the sea, but it is debatable whether West Thorney is really a village any more.

# 4

## *Around Chichester*

I FIRST visited Bosham when I was a very small boy, not yet of school age; we went by bus on that long route 31 which ran the length of the coast from Brighton to Portsmouth and Southsea, and I have a memory of a church surrounded by mud. At the age of three and a bit one can hardly be expected to appreciate either historical associations or ancient buildings and I did Bosham—pronounced Bozzam—less than justice. It is one of the best known and best loved spots on the whole of the south coast but it is nevertheless true that at low tide there really is a great deal of mud.

Bosham's history is long and splendid. It was settled by the Romans—there is a tradition that the Emperor Vespasian lived here at a place known as Stone Wall—and many Roman relics have been discovered over the years. Between the retreat of the Romans and the establishment of Saxon rule Christianity virtually disappeared from the south-east of England. It was kept alive, as the Venerable Bede records, by "A certain monk of the Irish nation, by the name of Dicul, who had a very small monastery in the place called Boshanhamm, a spot surrounded by woods and sea". For a time in the tenth and eleventh centuries Bosham was a place of world importance. It is generally believed, although without any firm evidence, that King Canute lived here; it is certainly true that the great Earl Godwin lived in Bosham, as did his son Harold. The Bayeux Tapestry includes a record of Harold at prayer in Bosham church before setting sail to negotiate with William in Normandy. A good deal of Bosham church is Saxon and legend has it that Canute built it in the early eleventh century. This may well be true for it is almost certain that his daughter is buried at Bosham. She died at the age of eight, and in 1865, in order to test the long-held local belief that her grave was in the church, the vicar had the supposed site excavated. He not only found a stone coffin of the eleventh century but in it were the remains of a child of approximately eight years. Nearly a hundred years later a second coffin was discovered which contained bones thought to be those of Earl Godwin.

Bosham today is a carefully preserved village; the green between the waterfront and the church is the property of the National Trust, the shops, cottages and houses are neat and picturesque. Its ancient seafaring traditions continue, for the headquarters of the training schooners *Winston Churchill* and *Malcolm Mitchell* are here and yachts and various small craft are packed tight at the moorings to the west and south of the village.

Across the creek is the much smaller village of Chidham situated, like Bosham, on a peninsula and the best part of four miles from the open sea. On the opposite side of the peninsula is Fishbourne, a main-road village which of late has become famous in a rather remarkable manner. Like Bosham it was known to have Roman associations but nothing more than fragments of Roman pots and building material had been found until one day in 1960 a workman engaged on digging a trench for a water-main in a field in the village unearthed what was obviously very ancient building rubble. He was sufficiently interested to get down off his excavator and take a look; he summoned his foreman and he in turn called in the Chichester Civic Society and then the Sussex Archaeological Society. Extensive excavations began and by the end of the year there lay revealed the remains of a palace covering upwards of ten acres. Many digs have since taken place, each one revealing more of the palace.

A record of the first ten years has been published by the professor in charge, Barry Cunliffe of Southampton University, under the title *Fishbourne, a Roman Palace and its Garden*. It tells, with all the merits of a good detective story, how the history of the palace, which was erected around A.D. 75 and destroyed some 200 years later, was deduced from a mass of fragments of broken tiles, mosaic, masonry, pottery and coins. Fishbourne is open to the public for most of the year and attracts thousands of visitors. No attempt has been made to reconstruct the original buildings; instead something rather like a school has been erected which exactly follows the footings of the north wing and enables visitors to obtain a close view of the mosaic-covered floors by means of walk-ways suspended a few inches above them. Complete restoration has been confined to the gardens, which has been made possible by analysing the various layers of soil and their positions. Nothing like it exists elsewhere in Britain, nor indeed is there anything exactly comparable in any part of what was once the western part of the Roman Empire.

The creeks and channels upon which West Thorney, Chidham, Bosham and Fishbourne stand are known collectively as Chichester Harbour, Fishbourne being but a mile from Chichester. The southern and eastern extremities of the harbour are formed by the Selsey or Mahood peninsula. Less than forty years ago it was possible to write of this, as E. V. Lucas did, as being "the part of Sussex most neglected by the traveller". It is rather different now, and of the seven communities defined at that time by the *Sussex County Magazine* as villages, one, Selsey, is certainly a town and others have become resorts, although we may still call them villages. Not only has the holiday-maker discovered the Selsey peninsula but the area has become popular with those who work in Chichester and further east and west along the coast towards Portsmouth, Bognor and Littlehampton. Every evening there are steady streams of traffic heading south along the two roads which lead down the peninsula from Chichester.

That said, Apuldram, the first village out of Chichester on the road to the Witterings, nevertheless consists of little more than two houses and a church, set amongst open fields. The outlying houses of Chichester are clearly visible a couple of fields away north-east of the church but St Mary the Virgin itself is quite isolated. It is a small church with a fine thirteenth-century chancel and a handsome fifteenth-century oak screen. The organ was built for Prince Albert and installed in the chapel at Windsor; it was later at Littlehampton before coming to Apuldram.

From the church a path leads through an archway of trees to a road which once continued to Apuldram harbour; the ever-changing coastline brought about its decline and in the seventeenth century it was replaced by Dell Quay, a half-mile to the south-west. Now the road serves only the church and two houses, the seventeenth-century manor and the former manor, Rymans, the oldest part of which was built by William Ryman in 1410.

Apuldram combines with Donnington, a mile to the east on the Chichester to Selsey road, to form one parish, although each has its own church. Holy Trinity, Donnington, dates from the thirteenth century but a severe fire in 1939 destroyed a good deal of it although it has been carefully restored. Hunston, immediately to the east of Donnington, and the Mundhams on the road to Pagham and Bognor, are both bigger than either Apuldram or Donnington with a good deal of recently erected houses, reflecting their proximity to Chichester. The road from Hunston to North Mundham runs parallel to the overgrown Portsmouth and Arundel Canal, which at one time formed part of a through water route from the coast to London. There are further sections of canal at Donnington and immediately to the east of Hunston, as well as the canal basin beside the railway station at Chichester, reminders of the early years of the nineteenth century when a flourishing traffic was carried on the network of canals around Chichester. Its heyday was brief, and unlike the industrial midlands and the north of England business was never so good in the south-east that canals and railways could co-exist for any considerable time. Relics of the Sussex canals remain although there has been little attempt at restoration; perhaps the most famous reminder is Turner's painting of the Chichester Canal in the Tate Gallery.

The churches of Hunston and North Mundham are both largely the work of the Victorian architect A. W. Blomfield. A picture of St Ledgers, Hunston, as it was before its restoration hangs in the church just inside the doorway. It suggests that whilst the present building may not possess any especial architectural merit it is nevertheless a good deal less primitive than it once was. When I visited it, it was being got ready for Christmas and looked cheerful and welcoming. Outside, beyond the duck pond and the plain stone and brick seventeenth-century Manor House opposite, the grey, brown and drab green landscape lay still and damp beneath a pale grey sky. There was little wind about and it was not cold for mid-December; a subtle feeling of nostalgia hung in the air, unimaginable when the holiday-makers and day-trippers are out in force in the summer but which will be familiar to those who know the countryside in winter.

Apuldram and Dell Quay are evocative names conjuring up idyllic scenes of autumnal plenty. It is a not inaccurate picture of the former, *apulder* being the Old English for apple, *ham* for an enclosure, and to this day it remains excellent apple-growing country. Dell Quay, however, is more water than dell, particularly at high tide. Within living memory it handled a considerable amount of commercial traffic for Chichester and as late as the turn of the century boats of up to 300 tons called carrying grain, building materials and shingle. By the 1930s road competition, allied with the more sophisticated facilities of the Solent ports and Littlehampton, had ended this, but there was compensation in the growth of pleasure boating, a feature characteristic of the entire coastline from Chichester westwards into Hampshire. An old store on the north side of the quay, which dates from pre-yachting days, is now the home of the Dell Quay rescue boat and the Sailing Club workshop. On the waterfront is the Crown and Anchor public house, whilst opposite it is the entrance to Dell Quay House with its gate-house beside it.

The only southward exit from Apuldram and Dell Quay, other than by water, is to return to the A286. This leads to Birdham, a straggling sort of village, stretching from the main road to the waterside. A good deal of it dates from the present century, although the parish of Birdham and West Itchenor goes back at least to Norman times and celebrated its 800th anniversary in 1975. Birdham and West Itchenor are both, like Dell Quay, yachting centres, although unlike it they have large permanent populations.

Birdham was still something of a quiet backwater until the late 1930s, and until 1936 it possessed a tide mill, the last working one in the county. The family of the last miller, the Farnes, had been associated with it almost since its erection in 1768. In 1936 it was taken over for the use of the yachting fraternity. The parish church of St James is a large stone church, heavily restored in the nineteenth century, although retaining its original sixteenth-century tower. In the churchyard is a huge yew tree, the tallest I have come across in Sussex.

West Itchenor's church, St Nicholas, is very much smaller, too small for there to be any division between the chancel and the nave. It is largely thirteenth century. The waterfront at Itchenor is rather similar to that at Dell Quay but the village is a good deal bigger, consisting of an almost mile-long road of modern houses and cottages, linking the A286 with the village street, which dates chiefly from the eighteenth century. The houses at the southern end are beautifully kept, with large gardens, whilst the flint cottages are very picturesque. One, with little else to distinguish it, bears the coat of arms of Her Majesty's Customs and Excise Service. At the end of the street, facing the waterfront and Bosham, is the Sussex Constabulary Marine and Harbour Master's Office. The fortunate Harbour Master looks out over one of the most pleasing prospects imaginable, with scores of yachts and other small craft in the foreground at anchor and moving up and down stream. On the far bank scattered houses stand amongst the trees, whilst forming a backcloth some half-dozen miles distant are the South Downs extending from west of Goodwood to the Hampshire border. Until the RAF vacated its base at Thorney Island in the summer of 1976 there seemed seldom to be a time when one of the Hercules transport aircraft was not circling around and one could look westwards and actually see the planes taking off and landing three miles away, but they were not especially noisy and were for long an accepted and unobtrusive part of the scene.

By retracing our steps from West Itchenor to the A286 we finally come to West Wittering, the most south-westerly point in Sussex. Ian Nairn refers to West Wittering as "posh" and East Wittering as "plebeian" and one can see what he means. To most visitors this is immediately brought home by the car-parking charges which in West Wittering are a cool 50p, whilst in East Wittering they are 14p (20p on Sundays and Bank Holidays). The attendant at East Wittering put the considerable difference down to his park being council property, but one feels that basically West Wittering likes to keep itself to itself. It is very difficult to gain access to the sea and the lane which leads to the church has double yellow lines painted along its entire length. It is perhaps fairer to say that West Wittering discourages the motorist for there is a good bus service to and from Chichester and if one cares to walk rather than park in the village then one is certainly welcome.

East Wittering delights in visitors and has a car park so large its attendant had only seen it full half-a-dozen times in the previous three years. As car parks go it is rather attractive, a large field with lavatories and a small shop which sells various not entirely expected commodities, including secondhand books. It is a short walk to the shingle beach and from there one may look eastwards past the entrance to Chichester Harbour and Hayling Island to the chimneys and tower blocks of Portsmouth, and southwards across the Solent with its great forts which resemble Dreadnoughts seen bow on, to the hills of the Isle of Wight.

Between the two Witterings is the prominent landmark of the tower of Cakeham Manor House. It is built of brick and dates from the sixteenth century, whilst the rest of the building is a mixture

of medieval, Tudor and Georgian. It used to belong to the Bishops
of Chichester and by the early sixteenth century had fallen into
ruins, but was restored by Bishop Sherborne. He was a man of great
zeal who reformed his diocese and was said to be "a terror to the
indolent". In between tours literally putting the fear of God into
slothful members of his flock, he rested at Cakeham (Cackham)
and planned his next campaign.

There are a few caravans at West Wittering and many more at
East Wittering, as well as chalets and bungalows, which continue
for four miles along the shores of Bracklesham Bay to Selsey. Yet
for all its twentieth-century appearance this section of coastline
has probably more historical associations than any other comparable length in the county. The Roman general Vespasian landed
here from the Isle of Wight on his way to Regnum and the straight-
est section of the West Wittering to Chichester road is known as
the Roman Road. Four hundred years later the Saxon invasion of
Sussex began at West Wittering when Aella and his three sons
landed with their army at a point known as Ella Nore.

In A.D. 661 King Aethelwalch was baptized by Wilfrid, Bishop
of York, and the Bishop was given all the land of the Selsey peninsula. Much of it remains church property today, whilst Wilfrid,
of course, became the patron saint of Sussex. In the charter containing this grant is the first mention of Wittering, or Wihttringes.
A cathedral was built somewhere to the south of the present
coastline but was abandoned in the eleventh century in favour of
one at Chichester, which city had by then recovered the status it
held in Roman times. The southern end of the Selsey peninsula had
meanwhile declined not only in importance but in actual size. The
entire Sussex coastline has been and still is constantly changing,
and in parts the prevailing winds and tides have bitten deep into
it, whilst elsewhere the sea has retreated leaving once flourishing
ports stranded some distance inland. Nowhere has the sea's hunger
been more voracious than around the Selsey peninsula and Wilfrid's
cathedral. The fields around it and entire villages have been inun-
dated and eventually quite covered over so that they now form part

of the sea bed. From time to time blocks of Caen stone from the old cathedral are washed up, and in the 1920s the owner of one of the first bungalows at Pagham collected enough pieces to outline his plot.

Bungalow building began here after World War I. Before then cars were rare enough to be objects of curiosity and a narrow, rickety bridge on the main road did nothing to encourage them. The principal form of mechanized transport in the early years of the twentieth century was the Hundred of Mahood and Selsey Tramway. It was one of a number of light railways owned by Colonel Stephens (another was the Kent and East Sussex which still survives). They were managed on a shoe-string budget and operated by second- third- and fourth-hand engines and carriages of great antiquarian interest and surprising effectiveness. But there was a limit to the enterprising Colonel's resourcefulness and in 1935 the Selsey tramway passed away, done to death by the motor car and the Southdown bus. By then there were hundreds of caravans and bungalows along the coast and their numbers were increasing daily. They are seldom beautiful, either individually or *en masse*, although their owners might justifiably claim that it is merely fortuitous that yachts, which at this time were taking up just as much of the scenery around the peninsula, are considered easy on the eye whilst caravans and chalets are not.

One of the biggest problems they brought with them was the disposal of rubbish. Previously the population of the Witterings had been small enough for each householder to make his own arrangements, as in other country areas, and in East Wittering bins along the cliff were emptied by a committee. However, the growth of the bungalow village made this too big a job for a small group of local people and it was suggested the Rural District Council took it on. Everyone would then pay rates, but the snag about this arrangement was that not everyone would get their rubbish cleared for some who thought they were in East Wittering were actually in West, which latter is a big, scattered parish. Consequently it might well happen that people who could afford a summer bungalow home as well as a permanent one elsewhere would benefit whilst the original farm labourer inhabitant might not. The problem was finally solved by the formation of the East and West Wittering Sanitary Committee, to which householders paid 17s. 6d. per annum, weekly wage-earners 7s. 6d. Rubbish was disposed of in an incinerator and the Ecclesiastical Commission, which owned the foreshore, looked after the bins along the beach. All this is, of course, history now, but it illustrates the problems expansion in the country brought, not solely to seaside villages but to inland ones too. A writer in the *Sussex County Magazine* at this time suggested that villages got together to solve the rubbish dispersal problem, perhaps by making use of disused pits or filling in marshy ground, and thus put an end to "hedges decorated with old kettles and ditches filled up with corned-beef tins and broken bottles".

A further threat to West Wittering in the 1930s was a harbour reclamation scheme whereby it was proposed to fill in a large area of the foreshore and make a harbour and golf course out of it. First mooted in 1934, discussions were still rumbling on in 1936. The locals were greatly opposed to it, claiming it would "ruin the place for birds and inhabitants", and eventually it came to nothing.

West Wittering must indeed have been transformed since the boyhood days of one of its oldest inhabitants, William Robinson. In 1935 he celebrated his ninety-sixth birthday and his seventieth wedding anniversary, and had never slept outside the parish. He worked all his life on the same farm, and had once travelled on a train, to Portsmouth. Since the 1930s the changes have been less dramatic and the street leading down to West Wittering church, with its flintstone cottages, seems hardly to have been touched by the twentieth century, although its immaculate condition is in fact the result of a lot of careful restoration.

Flint is used in great quantities on the Selsey peninsula, as is thatch, for schools and other public buildings as well as for houses and cottages. The church of St Peter and St Paul, West Wittering, is built of rubble, flint and beach boulders, successor to a Saxon church erected on the site around A.D. 740. The oldest part of the present church dates from Norman times, all that is except for "one precious fragment" to quote W. E. P. Done's guide to the church. This fragment is a cross cut into stone, discovered during restoration of the church in 1875, and reckoned by C. A. Ralegh Radford, formerly Inspector of Ancient Monuments, to have very likely been the gable cross of the monastery church of 740. For seven centuries prior to its discovery a hundred years ago it lay hidden, embedded in the masonry of one of the walls, and is now displayed in a cabinet in the west wall of the side chapel.

Earnley, half a mile inland from East Wittering, is, like Apuldram, hardly large enough to be a village. It possesses a thirteenth-century church with a cluster of houses around it, a windmill to the north at Somerley and very little else other than farms and fields. The last two villages of the peninsula, Church Norton and Sidlesham each lie beside Pagham or Selsey Harbour, the former at the south-west corner, the latter at the north-west. Pagham is a couple of miles away to the east and ought really to be included with them; one hesitates to do so only because, although so close, the many streams and inlets make a detour of ten miles necessary in order to reach it.

Church Norton is a very small community with a church which is built on the site of St Wilfrid's original monastery. It is thirteenth century and was once much larger, but in 1864 all but the chancel was removed and rebuilt to form the parish church of St Peter, Selsey. It stands close to where Pagham Harbour meets the sea. In June 1975 a pilgrimage took place from Wilfrid's chapel at Church Norton to Chichester to mark the ninth centenary of the removal of the cathedral from Selsey to Chichester.

Sidlesham (originally Siddlesham and still pronounced that way) is the largest inland village of the peninsula. It is made up of a number of hamlets spread along, and to the east of the Chichester to Selsey road, the principal part of the village being just north-west of Pagham Harbour. From it a lane lined with some attractive

E

cottages leads to the Old Mill Farm and the Old Mill House and the harbour. This latter is a haunting place with an air of wild desolation which it retains even on the hottest weekends when the nearby beaches are thronged with bathers and every caravan and chalet occupied. It was declared a nature reserve in 1964 under the ownership of the Sussex Water Authority, for whom it was to be managed by West Sussex County Council, and it will remain a sanctuary for wildfowl and waders, a breeding place for little terns, and a home at various times of the year for 260 species and races of birds in all. Porpoises have been seen in the harbour and occasionally dolphins and grey and common seals approach its mouth. At low tide the view from the old mill at Sidlesham is of an expanse of mud flats interspersed with gulleys, at high tide it is of 1,500 acres of water.

The harbour has an interesting history, being at one time a port for sea-going craft. Gradually it silted up and in the nineteenth century a wall was built cutting it off from the sea. Then on the morning of 16th December 1910 a combination of heavy rain and an unusually high tide broke the wall down and once again Pagham had a harbour. It has remained in this state since then, although the draught is sufficient to permit only the smallest craft.

The irony of the contrast between the boom in holiday homes and sailing for pleasure on the one hand and the severe unemployment and desperate living conditions in other parts of the country did not go unnoticed and in 1936, 289 acres of farmland were purchased at Sidlesham by the Land Settlement Association. This charitable body had been set up to provide a new start for unemployed men and their families in various parts of England and forty such families were brought to Sidlesham. They were trained in various aspects of farming and horticulture, each man having approximately four acres, and their produce was sold through the co-operative which was careful to market it nationally so that established patterns of local trade would not be upset. By the end of the year the Association owned 800 acres and in 1937, 10,000 bacon pigs and millions of chrysanthemums and eggs were produced. All the men were former miners; almost all were delighted with their new life. Whilst many are now dead or retired, some still live in their distinctive houses set amongst the greenhouses and fields and plots along the Selsey to Chichester road and the Association continues to flourish.

Pagham, across the harbour from Sidlesham, has become part of Bognor, but behind the chalets which line the beach as far east as the lagoon and continue almost up to the harbour's edge, something of the old village remains. One cannot imagine that the building of bungalows right up to the shingle would be tolerated today; practically all date from before World War II and a good many are actually old railway carriages, albeit heavily disguised and added to. To the north of them along a lane which leads down to the harbour are some old cottages and the stone-built parish church of St Thomas à Becket, which goes back to the early days of the Conquest. Thomas à Becket had a palace here, of which the moat remains, whilst the remnants of a medieval rectory are incorporated in a farm. Barton, at Nyetimber just north of Pagham, is a manor house which is now a farm. It contains sections of pre-Norman walling and gabling and the Rev. A. A. Evans suggests that it is probably the oldest continually lived-in house in the county.

The church has some interesting stained glass. That in the lancets at the east end is sixteenth century and comes from a church in Rouen, whilst the rose window in the west end was put in as a thanksgiving for the recovery from illness of George V. He stayed in a now demolished house within the ancient boundaries of Pagham when convalescent in 1929, although Bognor usually claims the distinction and the suffix 'Regis'. It is less inclined to broadcast the remark said to have been made by the King on his deathbed. As he lay dying, one of those present, by way of encouragement, suggested that he would soon be well enough to once again visit the resort; the King is alleged to have replied, "Bugger Bognor."

The group of villages in the area bounded by the A259 Chich-ester to Bognor road, the A27 Chichester to Arundel road, the River Arun and the coast share one significant feature: each is built on completely flat land. Almost the only variation from the level anywhere is the bridge under the railway at Barnham. Inevit-ably there is a certain lack of variety about them and some suffer the additional disadvantage of being rather too close to Bognor and affect a suburban air. But there are others which lie deep in the countryside and have a good deal to commend them.

Oving, two miles from the centre of Chichester, is an attractive village, quite large and compact with a variety of old and new buildings which use many different materials, although flintstone predominates. The church of St Andrew is almost completely of the thirteenth century, despite being much restored in the mid-nine-teenth. It stands beside a mushroom farm and opposite some flint almhouses which date from the time of the church's restoration and, as I write, are being extensively rebuilt.

A few hundred yards north of Oving is the western extremity of Tangmere aerodrome, and beyond this Tangmere village, the spire of Oving church being a prominent landmark in the view south from Tangmere. There is a church of St Andrew here too, which must cause some confusion as the two villages, with Box-grove, make up one parish. The Tangmere St Andrew's is largely twelfth and thirteenth century, although it contains fragments which may be a good deal older. There are some reused Roman bricks, a stone font which is probably from the Bracklesham beds now under the sea, and a small window on the south side with a bas-relief sculpture which may be from the lost Selsey Cathedral. Its design is indistinct but it has been suggested that it is the head of John the Baptist being presented by Salome. Outside the porch is an ancient yew with a trunk so hollow that the church-yard roller is kept in it. A number of the graves are of an unusual hump shape, as though the ground was too hard for the coffin to be buried deep in it, and made of bricks. There are some similar

ones in neighbouring churchyards but none that I have seen beyond
the immediate district.

Tangmere aerodrome was constructed by the RAF in the early
1930s and a good many buildings arrived with it, including
married quarters in typical Air Ministry red brick. Tangmere was
one of the Battle of Britain stations, although it is very quiet
today.

Adjoining the south-eastern corner of the aerodrome is Alding-
bourne, a small village with a neat group of houses, all on the same
side of the road, facing eastwards across open grassland, with the
rebuilt Norman church of St Mary at the southern end of the
village.

Westergate is a good deal larger and more modern. It stands
at the junction of the Chichester to Littlehampton and London
to Bognor roads and has grown greatly in the present century,
stretching out to join Eastergate, which in turn has linked up with
Barnham. In the village centre is a public house with the curious
name 'Labour in Vain' and a sign depicting a woman scrubbing
a black baby. The story goes that an eighteenth-century owner of
the inn, then a private house, went to live in the tropics and when
his wife returned, before him, she gave birth to a coloured child.
In later years the 'Labour in Vain' came into the ownership of the
Ecclesiastical Commissioners, who primly changed the name to the
New Inn. The old name was restored in 1927.

Eastergate has a pleasant main street and a village hall with
murals by Byam Shaw, but its focal centre is really Barnham, which
is almost a small town complete with substantial Victorian and
Edwardian villas. The centre of the village is the railway station,
the cause of its importance, being the junction of the Bognor and
Chichester and Portsmouth lines. Although Barnham is largely
modern its name is Saxon, meaning the settlement of Beorna, a
follower of Ella. The church of St Mary is partly Norman, whilst
nearby is the fine brick Barnham Court Manor house which was
built in the early seventeenth century. There is an old windmill at
the east end of the village on the main road, which still be-

longs to a miller and corn merchant, John Baker. It worked until the early 1930s and although the sails have been taken away the mill remains in use as a store and milling continues on the site.

North of Barnham and just off the A27 is Walberton, not perhaps as picturesque as Amberley, Bury or Lindfield, but handsome and scrupulously looked after, as its award for the Best Kept Large Village in West Sussex indicates. It is a big village with a long, winding main street which contains a great variety of ages and styles of houses, cottages, shops and other buildings. There is a good deal of flint and some brick and what was once a large and beautiful timber-frame house which, when I last visited Walberton, had been almost completely destroyed by fire. The parish church of St Mary stands at the east end of the oldest part of the village, close to the elegant white stucco Walberton House in 1803, south of the main street.

St Mary's was heavily and not very sensitively restored in the early part of the present century, but still has a good deal to commend it. There is a very old stone font and an equally ancient stone coffin which was dug up in the churchyard in 1834. Coffins were seldom or never made of stone after the thirteenth century. Dating from this century are a memorial tablet on the north wall by Eric Gill and a memorial window in the south aisle to Lord Woolton. This window depicts in a colourful and pleasing manner episodes from Lord Woolton's life, including unemployed dockers in Liverpool in the 1930s, whom Lord Woolton attempted to help, St Paul's during the Blitz in World War II when Lord Woolton was Minister of Food, barges and ships in the Thames, and various coats of arms associated with him.

Yapton is another village with a good deal of flint walls and houses, although it is by no means as neat as Walberton. It is on the opposite side of the railway line from Bognor and almost within sight of Bognor. Its church is its most distinctive feature, being essentially of the late twelfth and early thirteenth centuries with little later additions or restorations.

Ford was the site of the third aerodrome in this corner of Sussex, between the Downs and the sea. It is now an open prison, although the aerodrome buildings remain and dominate the skyline. On the opposite side of the road from the old runway and set some distance back in a field is the tiny church of St Andrew, standing amongst a clump of trees and with the Arun and the railway immediately behind. It and St Mary's, Climping, a mile away down the road to the south, are both of unusual interest.

St Andrew's is a simple building, with a pre-Conquest nave and a good deal else which is Norman. The guide book to St Mary's quotes the following words of a Victorian archaeologist: "Bosham for antiquity, Boxgrove for beauty, Climping for perfection." It is almost entirely of one period, the early thirteenth century, the only significant exception being the fine, massive tower which is some fifty years older and was probably, like those belonging to the churches alongside the Ouse between Newhaven and Lewes, once a watchtower. The walls are 4½ feet thick. There is a window in the church depicting St Paul, a reminder of the long-held belief that he visited Sussex following his meeting in Rome with Claudia, the daughter of the British chief Caractacus and wife of Pudens, commander of Regnum. A further link with the Holy Land is the Crusaders Chest, standing by the north wall of the chancel. It was ordered to be put in the church by Pope Innocent IV on the last day of A.D. 199 so that people would place in it their contributions to enable poor knights to go on a crusade.

Climping, or Clymping, village lies some way south of the church on the opposite side of the A259 coast road, on a lane which leads down to the sea. East of Climping, from the mouth of the Arun at Littlehampton eastwards there is continuous development, but Climping is untouched, the lane ending beside some thatched stone barns at the edge of the shingle beach. In winter it is a quiet, deserted spot, but on a Sunday afternoon in summer or at a Bank Holiday it is hardly possible to see the pebbles for people and the village street is overwhelmed by cars.

At the end of a drive just behind the beach is Baliffscourt, a rather remarkable building. It is now a hotel and in its present form dates from 1935. Baliffscourt is actually a group of buildings, a number of small houses and cottages which are either faithful reproductions in the medieval style or genuine medieval buildings transported from their original sites, and the main house. This latter is also medieval and is constructed out of what remained of the original Bailie's Court. This was primarily the chapel which had once belonged to the Abbey of Seez in Normandy. The land was granted to the abbot by the first Lord Arundel, Robert Montgomery, a warrior who loved a fight and was at Hastings but who later turned to founding monasteries and rebuilding churches with as great an enthusiasm as he had shown for bloodier deeds.

Boxgrove could do with a book all to itself for it is one of the great treasures of Sussex. The village, three miles north-west of Chichester and linked to Halnaker on Stane Street, is pleasant enough but there is nothing in it to compare with the Benedictine Priory, now the parish church of St Mary and St Blaise. Partly ruined, it dates back to c. 1115 when the land on which it stands was given to the Abbey of Lessay in northern France by Robert of Mortain and the daughter of the Earl of Arundel to mark their marriage. The church was built over a period of a hundred years and later additions were a sacristy and chapel in the fourteenth century. After the Dissolution the nave of the original church was let fall into decay and was partly demolished. Thomas de la Warr, direct descendant of the founders of the Priory, had to give it up but a good deal was preserved, including the early thirteenth-century choir which became the main part of the new church, the twelfth-century tower and transepts, the sacristy and the chapel, the latter becoming the new porch.

The ruins of the old church and the domestic buildings to the north stand amongst tombstones, undergrowth and long grass and have a romantic air, but those parts still intact are beautifully preserved. There are many carvings and the vaulting of the nave was painted by Lambert Barnard, one of the first English painters to whom we are able to put a name. He also worked at Chichester, Cowdray House and Amberley Castle, but the arms, crests and botanical signs at Boxgrove are considered to be his best work; he died around 1567.

After the Dissolution, Boxgrove and Halnaker were sold to the Morley family. In 1701 the estate passed to Mary Morley who married the Earl of Derby. She had homes for eleven women of the parish and of Lavant and Tangmere put up at Halnaker and she also founded a school; both foundations still exist. Her heir sold the estate to the Duke of Richmond, owner of the adjoining Goodwood Estate, and Halnaker House is now a ruin, although a new one of the same name was built by Lutyens in 1938. On a hill overlooking the village is one of the oldest surviving windmills in Sussex. It has a brick tower and dates from around 1750. In 1934 it was restored as a memorial to Lady Bird, wife of Sir William Bird of Eartham.

Stane Street, much the best-known Roman road in the county, forms the A285 from Chichester to Halnaker; beyond Halnaker the A285 swings slightly to the west but Stane Street continues for five miles over the Downs to the Roman villa at Bignor and this stretch has been described by I. D. Margary in his definitive work *Roman Ways in the Weald* as "the most perfect bit of Roman road to be found in Britain, much as the Romans left it except for the turf covering".

Southwards along Stane Street, and almost part of Chichester, is Westhampnett, a small village. It is the birthplace of the famous cricketer F. W. Lillywhite, and the site of a medieval leper hospital which later became a hospital for the poor, dedicated to Mary Magdalene. The north end of the village, where the A27 and the A285 meet, is still known as Maudlin. The parish church of St Peter contains some Roman brick, taken from the ruins of Regnum. A by-road from Westhampnett leads to Westerton, a hamlet bordering the former Goodwood car race track where the British Grand Prix used to be held. Now it is a research track and a landing place for light aircraft. Goodwood House is north-west of

Westerton, the famous horse-racing course on top of the Downs behind it.

Eartham, north-east of Halnaker and very close to the Downs is a tiny village belonging to the parish of Slindon. The church is in scale with the village and almost hidden by trees. Its exterior is largely nineteenth century but the interior has been much less restored and goes back to early Norman times. William Hayley, who was a friend of many of the prominent literary and artistic figures of his time and had them down to stay with him, lived at Eartham Hall from 1774 to 1820.

Slindon is a large, handsome, and rather quiet village, just off the A29 London to Bognor road. Many of the houses are of flint or brick and there is an almost comically picturesque thatched post office. Slindon is built in the shape of an uneven triangle, with some modern council houses down at the bottom end by the new school, the parish church of St Mary is near the top end on the west side, and beyond is the Roman Catholic church of St Leonard. Roman Catholic churches are not common in Sussex villages, although they are to be found in all the towns. St Leonard's was built in 1865, and with its plain, bright interior is a great contrast to the Norman St Mary's.

Slindon House was originally a palace of the Archbishops of Canterbury, although virtually nothing of this period remains, and Archbishop Stephen Langton died here in 1228. The House, which is now a school, Slindon Park, which stretches up the Downs to Bignor Hill, and a good deal of the village, all belong to the National Trust, which no doubt accounts for the excellent state of preservation.

In the church is the only wooden effigy in Sussex, a figure of Anthony St Leger, who in his will of 1539 directed that he be buried at Slindon. The left foot is mutilated but otherwise the striking and vigorously carved figure is complete. There is also a memorial to Richard Newland, "the father of modern cricket", a reminder that the village has a long cricketing tradition. In July 1914 Slindon played a match against Addington, Surrey, to commemorate their first meeting 100 years earlier. It was played under a clear, cloudless sky and during the afternoon three air-ships flew over on their way to join the Grand Fleet for a review at Spithead. From the review the ships and airships went off to take up battle stations for the First World War.

# 5

# From Arundel to Brighton

IMMEDIATELY north of Arundel are three of the loveliest of Sussex villages, Burpham, Bury and Amberley. Burpham—pronounced Burffam—is the least known and the least visited of the three for it lies at the end of a lane between the Arun and the Downs. It is reached from Arundel by a turning off the A27 Worthing road east of the station. One may walk to it in a leisurely hour from Arundel, but unless one chooses to go on a Tuesday or Friday one cannot reach it by bus. The road winds up and down following the course of the Arun for much of the way and then seems to be leading one away from the village before it swings sharply westwards and upwards to the church and the green. On this green in July 1876 a cricket team from Oxford University was playing the village, and at the tea interval the young men were discussing their future careers. One of the quieter members had to be pressed to commit himself; eventually he said, "I think I shall go back to the Cape. I think there is something to do over there." His name was Cecil Rhodes.

Burpham, despite its relative inaccessibility, is seen each day by thousands for it lies a few hundred yards from the Horsham to Arundel and Bognor railway line and passengers get a clear view across the water meadows of the church and the houses and cottages grouped around and beneath it. The grassy slopes around the green, conveniently close to the pub, provide an excellent venue for parties of hikers to take lunch, and the temptation must be great on a warm afternoon to spend the rest of the day there amongst the lush flowers, both wild and cultivated, which abound in Burpham, gazing out over the Downs and the river to the spires and turrets of Arundel. There is a good deal of flint and thatch in Burpham and the walls of the church of St Mary the Virgin are made almost entirely of flint rubble. The oldest of these walls, the north one, goes back to pre-Conquest days; most of the rest of the church is late twelfth and early thirteenth century. The restoration in the 1860s by Sir Thomas Graham Jackson was, on the whole, done rather carefully, although in the process some fragments of wall paintings were discovered and destroyed without any record of them seemingly being made.

Bury, the best part of five miles distant to the north-west, is very much better known than Burpham for it lies immediately beside the A29 Bognor to London road and a magnificent view is to be had of the village from Bury Hill as one descends the A29 from Arundel Park. The houses and cottages are grouped around the main street which descends gently from the A29, past the crossroads and down for a half-mile to the church and the river. It is not unlike Thakeham in that the houses and cottages are almost buried amongst trees, bushes and flowers with high banks forming a cutting. At the top of the street, above the crossroads, is Bury House, a handsome mansion of stone, timber and plaster, built in 1910 in the Tudor style, and the home in his later years of John Galsworthy. He wrote a good deal here and when *The Forsyte Saga* was televised the famous scene between Jon and Fleur was set, as in the book, on Chanctonbury, eight miles distant. Inevitably perhaps, the house opposite Galsworthy's old home is called the Forsytes, but no one has cashed in and started a tourist industry, which is as well for Bury is far too small to handle it and the carefully balanced character of the village would be destroyed. Bury House is now an old people's home. A much-loved radio personality whom listeners during the war years will remember, Mabel Constanduros with her Buggins family, also lived in Bury. Her home was at Prattendens Cottage, behind the Dog and Duck, and she took a great interest in local affairs, judging at baby shows, and winning prizes in knitting competitions, and she even had a lupin named after her.

The majority of the houses and cottages in Bury are built of sandstone. The church dates from the early thirteenth century with a shingled oak spire of 1603. Its four bells are all ancient, dating from between 1400 and 1625, but only one is sound. It is unusual to find that there are more names on the 1939–45 war memorial than there are on the 1914–18 one. The sanctuary lamp was given by the parents and brother of one of the 1939–45 victims, Harold Rafur. The road ends by the church but from there a footpath leads past willows to a bank protecting the village from the Arun. Delightful as is all of Bury, this part is the most picturesque of all, with the Downs and Amberley just across the river. There was a ferry connecting Bury and Amberley until fairly recent times, but as the signpost at the crossroads indicates it no longer operates.

The road from Bury to Amberley passes through Houghton, part of Amberley parish, crosses a stone causeway leading to Houghton Bridge, goes under the railway beside Amberley and Houghton station, and after bearing left and climbing the lower slopes of the Downs comes within sight of the village away to the north. Amberley has been called "The pearl of Sussex", the readers of the *Sussex County Magazine* in 1934 voted it the loveliest village in the county, and it is a favourite destination of coach tours, mysterious and otherwise. Fortunately not everyone's notions of perfection in villages coincide and there are no shortages of challengers for the title which is claimed for Amberley: it really all depends on what one is looking for.

Amberley's written history begins in A.D. 670 when King Cedwalla granted the lands at Amberley and Houghton to Bishop Wilfrid. Luffa, a successor to Wilfrid, replaced the original wooden church with a stone one about 1100, of which the present nave and chancel are part. One hundred years later another Bishop of Chichester, Ralph Neville, built a manor house at Amberley for use as a summer home. Towards the end of the fourteenth century it was fortified and the impressive remains of this are what we see today as Amberley Castle. The castle stands at the west corner of the village beyond the church, a great high cliff of rock guarding the village from possible attackers approaching from the river across the water meadows. These meadows gave rise to the old nickname Amberley Gonnolves applied to local people. It is said that a villager, when asked where he lived, would reply, "Amberley, where would you?" if it was summertime, but if it was winter his answer would be "Amberley, God Knows." Floods were so common in wintertime that Amberley people were said by their neighbours to have webbed feet. The river still floods and in 1937 the value of the land fell as a consequence from £5 to £1 per acre. The river has its compensations, of course, and Amberley trout are reckoned to be one of the four best Sussex fish, the others being Arundel mullet, Chichester lobster and Selsey cockles.

Amberley has long been as popular with artists as with anglers, and the scale of the village is small enough to provide the best of them with satisfactory subjects; although inevitably the emphasis over the years has been on scenes of rustic bliss with little hint of the flooded, ruined land and insanitary, overcrowded living conditions which were the other side of the picture. The most famous painter of Amberley is Edward Stott, a native of Rochdale, who settled in the village in 1885 where he remained until his death in 1918. His pictures in and around Amberley and of Amberley people were regularly exhibited at the Royal Academy, and after his death his studio became a museum and was visited by Queen Mary. Artist friends of his were commissioned to design a memorial and as a result Derwent Wood did the grave and F. Anning Bell a stained-glass window in the north wall of the church. From the same period there is a beautifully simple relief head, carved in memory of a seventeen-year-old girl who died in 1919.

Amberley is laid out, or rather has grown, roughly in the shape of a square, with the church and the castle to the north-west. The great charm of the village is in the juxtaposition of the thatched stone cottages, each beautifully cared for, and the trees and flowers which grow so liberally throughout Amberley. The road beside the church narrows to become a track descending steeply to the water meadows and continues beneath the castle walls towards the station and the site of the erstwhile ferry to Bury. Before the days of the railway and the motor car the cows grazing in the meadows would have been walked to market and as a consequence the village streets were liberally strewn with dung. Bullocks had to go to Barnham market, nine miles distant, whilst a trip to the annual sheep fair at Findon involved setting off with the flock at midnight. An Amberley farmer, Albert Johnson, recalling these long hours, nevertheless knew when to call a halt and remarked that throughout his farming life he "Never experienced a year when crops suffered any significant damage as the result of his refusal to work on Sundays."

Wilfrid Cheal in his book *Amberley Heritage* records the equally long hours worked by many other trades until fairly recent times. The Amberley postman, for instance, would begin his day at the Arundel sorting office at 5.30 in the morning, take a lunch break in a specially provided hut by the cricket field at Amberley in which there was a brazier and coal, and after collecting the second post from the station would eventually finish back at Arundel around 7 p.m. One of the places he would visit was Peppering Farm, up on the Downs between Burpham and Amberley. Even in those times in the early days of the motor vehicle, Sussex roads were nothing very marvellous, but at one time they had been a byword for wretchedness. Edward Lear stayed at Peppering House in 1829, and was so impressed by the awfulness of the roads he had to negotiate to get there that he sat down and wrote the following poem:

> If you wish to see roads in perfection,
> A climax of cart ruts and stones;
> Or if you have the least predilection
> For breaking your neck or your bones;
> If descents and ascents are inviting,
> If your ankles are strangers to sprains,

(*above*) Bury in late spring. (*below*) A variety of building materials and styles at Cowfold. (*overleaf*) Steyning, Bramber and Upper Beeding from the Downs

Slaugham, within a few hundred yards of the A23

Thakeham seen from the churchyard

(*above*) The village stores at Coolham crossroads. (*below*) Harvest Festival at West Chiltington. (*overleaf*) A view across the Cuckmere valley towards Milton Street and Berwick

Bignor

Ditchling, a culture-conscious village

If you'd cure a penchant for sliding,
Then to Peppering go by all means.

Immediately beyond the turning for Burpham on the A27 is
the A284 which leads to Littlehampton. It descends to the level
of the meadows beside the Arun and a mile north of Littlehampton makes a right-angle bend through the small village of Lyminster. The name would suggest it is of Roman origin although the
earliest record of its dates from A.D. 901 when it was bequeathed
by Alfred to his nephew Osfred. Despite its proximity to Littlehampton, which is but a field away, Lyminster possesses little
of the later nineteenth or the twentieth centuries. Most of its
houses are large, standing behind flint walls, and the village has
an air of exclusiveness unusual in one so near a seaside resort.

A Benedictine convent stood to the south of the church, where
there is now a farm: it was established some one hundred years
before the Conquest, whilst the church itself, which once belonged
to the nuns, came eighty years later. St Mary Magdalene is a
fine church with a good deal of Saxon work—principally the
walls of the nave and the chancel—the rest being largely Norman.
Two ancient tombs stand beside the twelfth-century Sussex marble
font and in one of them are the remains of a slayer of dragons.
He was either a knight or a local farmer's boy—there are two
versions of the story—and the dragon was supposed to have lived
in a pool, still to be seen in a field to the north-west of the
church. The pool, which is unusually deep and was for long
thought to be bottomless, is called the Nucker Hole. *Nicor* is
the Saxon word for sea-monster, which would suggest that the
story goes back to Saxon times and may not be as far-fetched
as one might first suppose. Beside the church is the Driftway, a
path which leads across the fields and the railway to the Arun
and to the site of the ford after which the village on the west
bank of the river takes its name. Cattle once used this route on
their way to market at Chichester.

From Lyminster the A284 continues over a level crossing and
into Littlehampton. Before entering the town proper a turning to

F

the left just beyond the crossing leads to what was once the village of Rustington but which is now suburbia with bungalows, caravan centres and an industrial estate. Adjoining Rustington is Angmering which, despite the suburban air its southern end effects, nevertheless remains a village with a good deal to commend it. Its northern end extends up the lower slopes of the Downs and clustered around its small green is a varied and attractive collection of buildings. There is a terrace of brightly painted cottages and beside them, opposite the church, a quaint Gothic stone and brick school of 1853 which has been skilfully converted into a library. Up on the hill beyond are some large, handsome houses, whilst the parish church of St Margaret is essentially Victorian, having been restored at the time the school was built; the only significant external original feature is the sixteenth-century tower. Beside it when I last visited Angmering stood the newly-completed Church hall. Even this has not entirely forsaken the Gothic style, with stones and brickwork matching the school.

The main road through Angmering, the A280, crosses the A27 coast road north of the village and then forms one of the finest routes through the Downs, linking up with the A24 immediately north of Findon. It sweeps across the southern edge of a fold in the Downs, affording a splendid view of Blackpatch Hill, and passes a house, built out almost into the road, which stood beside one of the last tollgates in the county. Immediately before this are lanes leading to the left and right to the twin villages of Patching and Clapham. Neither is especially picturesque or in any other noticeable way remarkable, but each possesses the un-self-conscious air of a village rooted in the land, the houses and cottages, mostly old but some new, built and adapted to suit the needs of their inhabitants and therefore each one different from its neighbour. Some are aesthetically more pleasing than others and at Clapham there is a small, modern development called Church Close and another under construction which are changing the character of the village but hopefully not transforming it, and in any case both villages are likely to remain small and to retain the feeling that they have somehow grown out of the land and are part natural, part man-made, like the fields and woods amongst which they stand.

Each village has a main street which leads nowhere other than up on to the Downs and a good proportion of the small amount of traffic which uses them is therefore agricultural. Both churches—the barn-like St John the Divine, Patching, and the pretty Blessed Virgin Mary, Clapham, skilfully restored by Gilbert Scott stand beside farms, there being a handsome typical Sussex wooden barn at Patching and a lovely but sadly derelict red brick and tile farmhouse at Clapham. Beside the wall of the churchyard at Clapham is a tombstone which until the restoration 100 years ago covered the grave of a priest in the chancel. It is extremely old and may indeed be that of the first parish priest, William de Radenore, appointed in 1257.

For 300 years, until 1800, Patching and Clapham were part of a huge estate which extended from Poling near Lyminster to Shoreham and which belonged to the well-known Sussex Shelley family. They lived at Michelgrove, to the north-west of Patching, in a house which was demolished after the Walkers, to whom the Shelleys sold the estate, had lost money in a variety of ways, one of which included the running of a stage coach between Worthing and London. In an attempt to gain an advantage over rival coaches the Walkers built the Long Furlong, now the A280, between Clapham and Findon. It hastened their downfall but at least we can remember them kindly for opening up to all a vista of the Downs.

Findon is a large village which has expanded greatly in the present century and the local flintstone no longer predominates, having been replaced as a building material by imported brick. It has a suburban air with avenues, some of them private, of detached villas just like those down by the sea at Ferring and Goring, nursing homes and corner shops. As at Sompting the church is some distance from the village, across the bypass on the opposite side of the valley. It and the handsome eighteenth-century Findon Place stand side by side in a secluded setting amongst the trees at the bottom of the Downs. The church of St John the Baptist, built entirely of flint, dates back to 1150 although much of it is more modern; there is, however, a very old and sturdy oak screen of the thirteenth century. St John's was extensively restored by Sir Gilbert Scott and is generally considered to have been one of the more successful Victorian efforts. The interior walls are largely unadorned although they were once extensively covered with murals, of which only a fragment survives. Around the arches the bareness of the white plaster is relieved by roughly shaped, subtly coloured, yellow-grey stonework. There is a memorial to a former chairman of the East India Company and "M.P. for London", George Lyall, who died in 1853, whilst on the west wall is a charming tapestry made by the children of Findon School in 1959 which depicts Wilfrid, Dicul, Cuthman and Caedmon and the events associated with them.

The suburban air of parts of Findon is counterbalanced by the proximity of the Downs and of the famous Neolithic flint mines at Cissbury, a few hundred yards away. The countryside is all around to the east, west and north and the village's continuing relationship with it is confirmed by the Southdown Sheep Fair which is held in Findon each September. In the 1930s when the village was expanding at a great rate and ribbon development threatened its independence, the fair was in decline. There were less sheep on the Downs and a seven-day week and low wages attracted few young men to the calling of shepherd. But after World War II there was a revival. There were 6,650 sheep at the 1949 fair and twice that number eight years later. The fair still flourishes today.

On the map, Sompting, like Durrington, High Salvington, and Lancing, appears to have been swallowed up by Worthing, but in reality, unlike them, it has managed to preserve a precarious independence. Not much more than a field separates the two but it is sufficient, and Sompting remains a small, compact village, with plenty of flintstone walls, a pub called 'The Smugglers', and a famous church. St Mary's lies on the lower slopes of the Downs, north of the village on the far side of the bypass. Surmounting its Saxon tower is a "Rhenish helm" roof, of a shape familiar in the Low Countries but unique in this country. It dates from around 1000, as do other parts of the church. St Mary's has a more than usually interesting history for in 1154 the Knights Templar took it over. They added to it extensively, one of their additions being the south transept which opens out of the main door and is at a lower level than the rest of the church. This is on account of its originally being the Templars' private chapel and separate from the rest of the building. The chapel was opened up for the use of all by the Templars' successors, the Knights of St John of Jerusalem; they built their own chapel on the north side. This became disused after the Dissolution and was restored only in 1971, eight years after the Order of St John resumed patronage of Sompting, following an absence of 430 years.

Washington, a village of narrow, winding lanes and, in spring and summer, flowers, lies over the Downs from Findon and Sompting, between the old and the new main roads. The A283 passes immediately to the north, meeting the A24 at a large roundabout and enclosing Washington within an uneven triangle, and ensuring that nothing but local traffic enters the village. It thus remains undisturbed, although far from sleepy, as a glance at the parish magazine will confirm. The parishioners contrive in their activities both to entertain themselves and to assist others. The annual flower show includes not only horticultural exhibits but ". . . Mr. Came from London with his Punch and Judy Show . . . the usual tombola, run as always by Miss Rona Offlow with enthusiasm and efficiency . . . children's sports . . . Shaylor's Funfare . . . busily making people sick . . . Mr. Cothard of Bramber with his smaller swings and roundabouts for the very young . . . and teas, an essential part of every Show". Washington, we are told, is "famous for its cake-making" and at the

August Bank Holiday weekend £12 was raised by selling teas to holiday-makers. These included a party of twenty young French people who were so refreshed "that they decided to walk back to Worthing". There is a summary of last month's weather and a list of forthcoming activities in the surrounding villages, amongst which are a savoury fish supper and a film show at Thakeham in aid of the Mission to Seamen, a Deanery Quiet Day at Upper Beeding and an account by the Vicar of Findon of his holiday in Oberammergau.

Findon stands beneath what is without doubt the most celebrated spot of the South Downs, Chanctonbury Ring. At 783 feet it is not quite the highest point on the Downs, but with its clump of beech trees it is the most clearly recognizable. The beeches were planted in 1760 by Charles Goring who lived at Wiston, an Elizabethan mansion to the east of Washington. He was then a young man and he lived to see his trees reach full maturity. A familiar and much loved landmark, they may be seen from the Brighton railway line north of Clayton, from Butser Hill in Hampshire, from Leith Hill in Surrey and from many other parts of Sussex and beyond its borders. Goring planted his trees inside the perimeter of an Iron Age hillfort which also contains the remains of a Romano-British temple.

The A283 continues eastwards from Washington past extensive sand quarries to Steyning, Bramber and Upper Beeding. The former two were for long important towns, Steyning being a port until the Adur silted up in the fourteenth century, whilst one of the five Saxon Rapes of Sussex was centred on Bramber. Steyning is still a town, although overshadowed by the growth of the seaside resorts on the other side of the Downs, but Bramber is now no more than a village. It has long been recognized as one of the most picturesque ones in the county and is well prepared for visitors with souvenir shops, at least one café which stays open on Sundays all the year round and restaurants. There is a fine view from the main street looking westwards to the parish church of St Nicholas which stands on a hillside with the ruined 76-foot high keep of the castle behind and above it. There are equally good views from the top of the mound on which the castle stands, eastwards beyond Upper Beeding towards the Devil's Dyke, north across the Adur Valley to the Weald, and south to Lancing College. A byroad leads over the Downs to Lancing and Sompting and at its summit immediately above Bramber one may look southwards and watch hang-gliders, triangles of brilliant colours, manœuvring gracefully against the cool green of the grass.

The castle belongs to Bramber's heyday, being built, like those at Arundel and Lewes, immediately after the Conquest to guard a gap in the Downs. It was destroyed by the Roundheads and all that remains are a few ruins and the extensive grass-covered site. The church, like the castle, was built by William de Braose. It was originally the chapel for a small community of Benedictines who, after a brief residence, transferred across the river to Beeding, leaving St Nicholas to serve the village and visiting seamen. The Knights Templar set up a house here and both King John and Edward I visited the town. But around 1350 a decline set in with the gradual silting-up of the river, and although barges continued to reach Bramber as late at the nineteenth century, by Elizabethan times it had ceased to be a port of any significance. It was inevitable that the church, standing so close to the castle, should be damaged when the latter was destroyed, and although it was patched up the poverty of the village militated against a thorough restoration. By the early nineteenth century Bramber was one of the rotten boroughs with thirty-five voters returning two M.Ps. The great reformer William Wilberforce once passed through the village, asked its name, and when told remarked, "How interesting, that is the place I am member for". Two of the last tollgates in the county were at Bramber and Upper Beeding, both closing in 1885. By then the railway had reached Bramber, bringing with it something of a resurgence. The line closed in 1966, save for the section from Shoreham to the cement works at Upper Beeding, leaving the main streets of both villages to cope with the heavy and increasing traffic between Guildford, Horsham and Shoreham.

Three tiny villages lie at the foot of the Downs on the byroad which connects the A2037 with the A23. The first, Edburton, possesses hardly sufficient dwellings for a hamlet, but for all that it has a church, and the next village, Fulking, belongs to its parish. The church was founded by Edburgh, the daughter of Alfred, around 950 and a good deal of the fabric goes back to that time, although essentially the architectural style of the church belongs to the thirteenth century, the old materials having been reused.

Fulking has to make do with a small mission church, but in other respects it is a good deal grander than Edburton with a post office, a tea room, and a pub, and a number of cottages and houses, many built of flintstone. The pub is appropriately named The Dog and Shepherd for it stands beside a fresh-water spring which at one time made the village a centre for sheep washing. The sports field opposite must be the most overgrown in the county, the grass being almost waist high except where a path has been beaten through to the swings. The slope of the Downs immediately above Fulking is precipitous, although horses somehow manage to graze on it, and from the field one's view to east, south and west is almost filled by a smooth expanse of green, interrupted only by curving paths of white revealing the chalk beneath the grass, the houses and cottages of the village at the very bottom.

From both Fulking and Poynings, the third of the three villages, the most prominent landmark on the Downs is the Devil's Dyke. Poynings is so close to the Downs that its parish church of Holy Trinity is built on their lower, wooded, slopes. The village takes its name from the Lords of the Manor, the Poyngges. Michael Poyngges, who built the beautiful, faintly neglected-looking church in the Perpendicular style in the late fourteenth century on the site of a Saxon one, fought at Crécy and Poitiers. The windows of Holy Trinity are all but entirely innocent of stained glass and the interior of the church is thus unusually light, despite the Downs filling the view through the handsome window over the altar. The few fragments of stained glass in the east window of the north transept are very old, dating back to the early fifteenth century. There is a memorial to the "eldest daughter of Thomas Lord Erskine, Lord High Chancellor of Great Britain". She also happened to be the wife of the rector, Dr Samuel Holland. He and his son Thomas, who succeeded him, were together in charge of the parish for eighty-one years, from 1807 to 1888, and they extensively restored the church which at the beginning of the nineteenth century was in a very bad state. The chapel was "dark and dank", three of the windows were blocked up and tombstones were uprooted and brasses stolen. Despite being wife and mother to these worthy churchmen, the Lord High Chancellor's daughter obviously valued her father's office above their achievements. For all the Hollands' long service it cannot compare with one of their eighteenth-century predecessors, George Beard, who was rector for no less than fifty-eight years. In all that time he is said to have restricted himself to but two texts, "Simon the Tanner" and "Felix troubled". Perhaps this explains the neglect Samuel Holland inherited. One can understand the reluctance of successive rectors to leave Poynings for it is a pretty village in as fine a setting as any in the county.

A steep lane winds around the edge of the churchyard, up the side of the Downs, joins the road from the Devil's Dyke close to what was once the village of West Blatchington, of which the principal unaltered remnant is the windmill, and so brings us by way of the Dyke Road into the heart of Brighton.

# 6

# *West of the Brighton Road,*
# *North of the Downs*

DESPITE the enormous amount of traffic the A23 London to Brighton road has always carried, even before the days of the motor car, its presence has had surprisingly little effect on the communities in its immediate proximity. The London to Brighton railway line, on the other hand, has transformed a number of places which lie on its route. Consequently nearly all the development south of Crawley has been to the east, the railway side, of the A23, and the area to the west is undeveloped, farming country with many scattered hamlets and a few villages.

Albourne is the first village on the A23 north of the Downs; only a few hundred yards of open country immediately east of the road separate it from the outskirts of Hurstpierpoint. It is compact and much of it dates from Victorian and later times, the thirteenth-century church being almost entirely rebuilt in the mid-nineteenth century. There is a handsome seventeenth-century house, Albourne House, to the south-west of the village and a fine Tudor one, Gallops, on the opposite side of the A23. Twineham, between two arms of the infant Adur, is hardly large enough for a village, but it has a main street leading past the school and ending at the early Tudor brick church which, when I visited it in early September, was beautifully decorated for harvest festival with a simple cross made of two runner beans pinned on the door. Back on the main road is Hickstead, which has a famous jumping course but which again cannot really be called a village.

Bolney is probably best known for its once dangerous cross-roads, where the A23 and A272 meet. Now a bridge carries the Brighton road traffic clear of the east–west traffic, although the latter is still likely to encounter delays at Cuckfield and Cowfold. The main street of Bolney runs parallel to the Brighton road, the older part of the village being at the south end around the church of St Mary Magdalene, a good deal of which is Norman. Buried in the churchyard is Henry Huth, a celebrated book collector whose collection, minus some fifty volumes which he left to the British Museum, fetched in 1910 the staggering sum of £300,000. The newer and largest part of Bolney is at the north end of the village and extends across to the A23.

Cowfold is the largest and most handsome village in the district. The A281 Horsham to Brighton and the A272 Winchester to Heathfield roads meet in its centre at a busy crossroads which makes life rather difficult for pedestrians at times, but the risk is worth taking for the best parts of Cowfold can only be appreciated on foot. To the east of the crossroads is the large green, bordered by fields, whilst on the opposite side is the church of St Peter with a lovely churchyard. Running along the northern edge of this are the backs of a delightfully varied row of houses and cottages built of red and grey brick, plaster, timber-framing and weather-boarding, roofed chiefly with red tiles. I once visited the church on a Saturday morning, a time when one can usually find the ladies of a Sussex village parish arranging the flowers. They will be only too happy to show one around the church and talk about the village, but sometimes one can be equally well entertained and informed by sitting quietly in a corner and eaves-dropping. It was thus possible to learn that the blackberries on the large bush in the churchyard were particularly fine that year and that one lady was a different person since "I've had my gall bladder removed". Beside the blackberry bush I found one of the churchwardens working on a painting of the church, the same churchwarden Mr Mills who had compiled and illustrated the guide. There are many memorials in St Peter's including a celebrated brass of 1433 to Prior Thomas Nelond of Lewes. It measures 10 feet 2 inches by 4 feet 3 inches, making it the largest in the county; unfortunately too many people had been given permission to make rubbings of it, even at £2 a time, and in August 1975 it was decided that the practice would have to stop owing to the damage caused. There is also a memorial to "Richard Pierce Gent" who "received a wound thro' his Body at Edgehill Fight in the year 1642 as he was loyally defending his King and country". Far from the wound proving mortal, Pierce lived on for another seventy-two years, dying at the age of ninety-four.

Also buried at Cowfold is Caroline Huddart, one of the pioneers of that cornerstone of village life, the Women's Institute. The WI actually began in Canada but the first English branch was founded in Sussex, at Singleton, in 1915 and the first chairman of the National Federation was a Sussex woman, Lady Denman. When Caroline Huddart died in 1932 there were some 200 branches in Sussex, more than in any other county in Britain.

A mile south of Cowfold can be seen the spire of what looks to be a large Victorian church immediately to the east of the main road. It is high enough to be visible a good way off and leads many people to assume that it must be part of a village, and it is therefore somewhat puzzling to find that it is in the middle of a wood. It belongs to the monastery of St Hugh, an enclosed Carthusian order which arrived at Cowfold from Paris just over 100 years ago.

South-west of the monastery is Partridge Green, a village which grew up in the late part of the nineteenth century around the now vanished railway. There is a trading estate on the site of the old station and a modern housing estate close by. A pub called 'The Partridge' stands on the corner where the B2116 which runs under the Downs through Hurstpierpoint and Ditchling to Lewes begins, next door to a sausage and pie factory.

Warninglid, north-east of Cowfold, has been a recent recipient of the Best Kept Small Village award for West Sussex and with its carefully placed and landscaped villas and houses and its neat brick church dating from 1935 it is easy to understand why.

Some four miles north of Bolney the A23 enters St Leonard's Forest. A short way inside, the dual carriageway crosses two handsome, pale-yellow stone bridges, although probably few motorists are aware of them as they sweep along the wide, tree-lined road towards Handcross. The lane which passes under the bridges links Staplefield and Slaugham. Staplefield, to the east, is a small village with a large, triangular-shaped green, a few houses and cottages, two pubs, the 'Victory' and the 'Jolly Tanner', and a church built in 1847. Unusually for a Victorian church it has a guidebook. It records that the clock was installed in 1877 in the hope that the local children would get to school in time; a short while later the Vicar found some of them firing catapults at it. There is a painting by Oliver Messel in the church which he had left half-completed as a boy at the family home, Nymans, near Cuckfield. After the fire in 1947 which destroyed a good deal of the house the picture was found undamaged; he completed it and his mother gave it to the church in 1958.

Slaugham, pronounced Slaffam, is as perfect an example as one could hope to find of a village quite untouched by the never-ceasing passage of traffic a few hundred yards away. It is a compact place of some twenty buildings, most of them situated in the main street which runs from the church to the gates of Slaugham Park. St Mary's, the parish church for Warninglid, Slaugham, Handcross and Pease Pottage, goes back to Norman times, although it was much restored in both the nineteenth and the early part of the present centuries. Its most interesting memorial is to Robert Ellison who died in 1839 at the age of seventy-one, having managed in that time to spend thirty-eight years as rector of the parish, thirty-four as rector of Southease, twenty-nine as curate of Bolney and forty-six as Canon of Wolverhampton. The cottages immediately beside the church are largely tile-hung but the main street, despite its diminutive size, encompasses a delightful variety of styles and materials. From its north end one may continue to walk for a half-mile through the grounds of Slaugham Park to Handcross, passing a seed merchant who also deals in clearing "lofts, sheds, garages, barns, and can offer a wide range of effects from postcards to pyramids (we are temporarily out of the latter)".

The track comes out by the A23 which at one time ran along the main street at Handcross but now cuts through and below it, a bridge connecting the older, smaller, western end with the largely twentieth-century eastern section. Pease Pottage, two miles to the north, is in complete contrast to Slaugham for it largely owes its existence to the main road. It is an untidy collection of houses, a corrugated iron church, and a garage. As at Handcross the A23 used to pass through it, but now Pease Pottage is perched above the intersection of the southern end of it and the London to Brighton motorway. From here one may look down the hill to Crawley.

In the five miles between Crawley and Horsham there are no villages, although the A264 which connects them and skirts the northern edge of St Leonard's Forest carries a great deal of traffic, as does the Crawley to Horsham railway line. Colgate, in the depths of the forest, is no more than a hamlet, and Faygate, despite a regular service of electric trains to and from London, is no larger.

Three miles south of Horsham on the A24 Worthing road is Southwater. It is a village which has grown enormously of late, becoming what is really a satellite of Horsham. Between 5 and 6 p.m. each weekday a cavalcade of cars and buses commutes from one to the other, although a good many of Southwater's inhabitants find employment in the village itself. They either work in the brickworks, which lie to the south of the disused railway line, or in one of the newly established light industries which have sprung up in Southwater. The new houses are nicely built in brick, but for a while Southwater is not going to be much to look at, especially whilst the unplanned muddle on the site of the old station persists and until the estates have mellowed and trees have grown.

Coolham is situated three miles south-west of Southwater at a busy crossroads where the principal inland road across Sussex, the A272 from Winchester to Heathfield and Hawkhurst, meets the Horsham–Storrington road. I once saw a Paris bus, presumably belonging to a preservationist rather than one which had taken a wrong turn at the Place Pigalle, negotiating Coolham crossroads, but despite such exotic sights the village remains quiet and in a sense out of the way, traffic notwithstanding. The only buildings in the village itself are a disused school, a pub, a large, white-painted shop and post office and some houses. In wilder days it was a haunt of smugglers, for they were common throughout the country, not merely in coastal areas, and in 1929 a horde of seventy empty wine-bottles was found in a cavity under a stone beneath the sluice of a water mill at Coolham. It was a perfect hiding place for within hours of being replaced the stone was once again covered with green slime.

Shipley lies south-east of Coolham and possesses one of the most magnificent windmills to be found anywhere. It stands to the west of the church, immediately beyond the modern vicarage. It is a very large smock mill, very nearly the biggest surviving one, and was partly restored by Hilaire Belloc who owned it and lived nearby at Kingsland from 1905 until his death in 1953. The mill's restoration was completed in Belloc's memory. The village is small and out of the way, although it has a long history, and in 1938 a pig farmer, digging for water, discovered fragments of Roman pots as well as layers of charcoal, wood ashes, and lumps of sandstone vitrified and contorted by great heat which indicated the presence of a charcoal-burning site. The parish church of St Mary the Virgin was built in the twelfth century by the Knights Templar on the site of a wattle and daub Saxon one and contains some fine unaltered features, in particular the windows, the chancel arches and the enamelled reliquary or portable shrine, all on the south side, which overlooks the Adur—here no more than a stream.

Ashington, four miles south of Shipley, is set astride the A24 London to Worthing road just north of the Downs and is consequently a busy place with a good deal of modern building. The largest part of the village lies on the west side of the road, as does the restored parish church of St Peter and St Paul. A lane leads due west from Ashington to Warminghurst, which consists of little more than the recently restored Early English church of the Holy Sepulchre, and an estate which once belonged to the Quaker William Penn. He held meetings at the nearby pub, the Blue Idol. Penn first went to Pennsylvania in 1684. The state had been given to, and named after, his father in payment of a loan of £15,000 to the Navy; apparently the Government thought it had got the best of the deal. William Penn returned to England in 1686 and around 1700 sold his estate at Warminghurst, moving to Rickmansworth where he died in 1718.

One of Penn's staunchest followers was Edward Woolven who, with his wife Jane, farmed two acres around the Friends Meeting House at Coolham. Woolven hardly ever left the village, one of the few occasions he did being in 1922 when at the age of eighty-seven he was taken by car to see the graves of William Penn and his children near Ricksmanworth. He described this outing as the "culminating joy in my life", and he died the next year, being interred in the burial ground beside the orchard at the Meeting House. At one period in his life Edward Woolven owned a duck which sat in its own chair beside the fire, a privilege it repaid by laying every day, without fail. This useful life was cut short by a fox and in compensation the local hunt sent Mr Woolven 2s. 6d. It was returned with the message that if that was all a duck which laid every day was worth he would rather do without.

The lane from Ashington to Warminghurst becomes a track and continues to Thakeham. This village, which is off the B2139 Storrington to Coolham road, can be idyllic, particularly on a

warm summer evening when the scattered cottages, lying remote
and silent amongst the deep hedgerows, appear to be on the
point of being engulfed by the luxuriant trees, shrubs and flowers
which surround them. The church of St Mary's is at the lower
end of the village but stands on rising ground above a pair of
half-timbered, plaster and Horsham tiled houses. Thakeham is
near enough to Horsham for a poster for the Capitol Theatre
there to be displayed on the village notice board, but it is even
nearer the Downs, and Chanctonbury dominates the skyline
south-east of the church.

St Mary's strikes one as being rather large for the needs of a
small village and in the past a number of influential families lived
in the parish. It is a solid, handsome church, the nave, chancel
and transepts dating chiefly from the twelfth century, built of
local sandstone and ironstone. The large fifteenth-century Perpendicular tower has a type of roof common in Normandy but
rare in England. The war memorial in the churchyard is unusual
in that it commemorates as many names from World War II
(twelve, including one woman) as it does from World War I. At
the other end of the village, on the main road, there are some
modern houses and a large nursery, and one of Lutyens' earliest
and best designs, Little Thakeham, of 1902–3.

West Chiltington, one mile west of Thakeham, is something of a
showpiece, a very pretty village which won the award for the best-
kept one in West Sussex for five years in succession, and about
which Lord Ponsonby wrote in the St Martin's review: "If West
Chiltington church were in Italy people would make pilgrimages
to it." Much of it belongs to the eleventh and twelfth centuries
and practically nothing is later than early seventeenth, the central
shingled spire dating from 1602. Murals cover a good deal of
the walls, the oldest of them representing a cross formed of an
endless rope, a design similar to one found at the Roman Palace
at Fishbourne. It must be close on 1,000 years old, being contemporary with the oldest part of the church.

In front of the churchyard wall are the old village stocks and

G

whipping post, restored in 1951 for the Festival of Britain; across the road is a small private museum. West Chiltington is far enough north of the Downs for flintstone to be a rarity, the houses and cottages in the attractive main street being chiefly of Green Burgate stone, with some brick and plaster. Many Sussex villages have grown considerably in the twentieth century, some to the extent that they have become towns, but West Chiltington is remarkable in that whilst the village itself has kept its character almost without alteration, there has been tacked on to it a large suburb a good deal bigger than the original village. This development lies to the south on the Washington road and comprises a great many spacious villas, houses and bungalows, many set in extensive grounds. The oldest go back to the mid-1920s when a collection of thatched houses of a vaguely Tudor appearance with exposed beams but with all the modern conveniences, including central heating, was put up by a local firm. They were carefully set amongst the woods and heather and the subsequent development has followed these lines the result being an atmosphere of discreet but unmistakable affluence. Standing above the newer part of West Chiltington is a partially restored black and white smock mill of around 1800; there is another mill a mile to the north-west by the tree-encompassed hamlet of Nutbourne.

If we head through Nutbourne we come out on to the A283 at Pulborough and then cross the Arun by the famous Stopham Bridge. This is the best known of all the lovely medieval bridges found in this part of the county. It dates from 1309 and was rebuilt in 1403. Six of its seven arches are original, the seventh being the raised centre one of 1822. Although narrow, the bridge manages to cope adequately enough with today's traffic and it is to be hoped that it will never be thought necessary to build a second bridge beside it for that would quite spoil the setting. The small village of Stopham and the attractive parish church of St Mary are set around a lane which runs parallel and to the west of the river.

North of Stopham, on the A272, is Wisborough Green, an appropriately named place for it possesses what must be very nearly the largest village green in the county, liberally planted with trees; a short distance away, by the pond, is another expanse of grass almost completely surrounding the church. The setting of the church is very fine, on rising ground, which the main road sweeps around. It dates from the thirteenth century, and apart from being a handsome building, contains much of interest. There is an unusually well preserved mural depicting St James and the Crucifixion, found in a recess by the chancel arch in the nineteenth century during restoration. Other paintings were discovered at the same time but it was not considered practical to preserve them. Then there is what is generally supposed to be a remarkably ancient altar stone which may predate Christianity and have been used for pagan worship on the hill where the church now stands. The north and south doors are very high for a village church, some 13 feet, and capable of allowing a man on horseback to pass through. The walls of this, the oldest, part of the church are unusually thick and it has been suggested that these features indicate that it was once a keep, guarding the river which flows nearby. Of the monuments perhaps the most interesting are two modern ones. The first is a lancet window made up of fragments of glass found locally and dedicated to the Huguenot glass-makers who lived in Wisborough Green in the late sixteenth and early seventeenth centuries. The second is the oak doors of the tower which are a memorial to those killed in the Dieppe raid in 1942. The raid was planned in Wisborough Green and carried out by the 2nd Division of the Canadian Army; the doors were given by the Home Guard.

The Home Guard was particularly active in Sussex during the 1939–45 War. The invasion was expected to take place along the length of the Sussex coast and indeed after the war captured German documents revealed that the first thrust would be to the ridge stretching from Hastings through Herstmonceux along the northern edge of the Hailsham marshes. The legendary

Warmington-on-Sea of 'Dad's Army' is clearly intended to be somewhere in Sussex, although not any specific resort; no doubt it is no more than coincidence that Pike is the name of the youngest member of the fictional Warmington-on-Sea Home Guard and also of the first commander of the real West Sussex Home Guard. Lt.-Gen. Montgomery, as he then was, took a special interest in the Sussex Home Guard which, with all other forces in the area, was under his command, and in 1942 he organized a combined training fortnight with the regular army at Amberley. By the beginning of 1944 the Home Guard began to take over all coast standing patrols, which meant 400–500 men on duty at any one time, 3,500 being involved altogether. The Sussex Home Guard was stood down at ceremonial parades throughout the county in December 1944.

Fittleworth can be reached from Wisborough Green by way of a lovely winding lane, through thickly wooded countryside, dipping down into the village past the gates to a large Georgian house, and ending at the crossroads by a cottage which was once an inn. This latter stands on a blind corner on the busy A283 Guildford to Shoreham road and it is just as well it no longer sells alcohol—I shouldn't imagine anyone who allowed his wits to become befuddled would last very long, for traffic whips around the corner and only the most agile of pedestrians should attempt to cross at this point. Fittleworth is almost two villages; the northern part up on the A283, clustered around the church, and the rest, which makes up the larger mark, spread out below along the Petworth to Arundel road. Fittleworth is a picturesque village and consequently has attracted many artists: the Swan Inn, a rambling place, is full of pictures. The most famous artist to visit the village was Constable, who stayed here and sketched in the vicinity. Tourists come to Fittleworth in some numbers and within twenty minutes one Saturday lunch-time three drivers stopped their cars beside me and asked directions, one the chauffeur of a Rolls who wanted the Swan. St Mary the Virgin, set on the highest point of the ridge on which the upper part of the village is built, is a lovely, largely sandstone church. The oldest part is the tower, dating from around 1200, with a typical broach spire. The old timber-framed nave was pulled down in 1870 and replaced by one in the style of the rest of the building, but which is generally considered to be inferior to it. The pews retain their candlesticks which are still used at Christmas Eve and Epiphany. Amongst the stained-glass windows are some by Kempe, who did so much work in Victorian times; it is unfortunate that he had such an unadventurous colour sense, although in this he was no worse than most of his contemporaries. Indeed the amount of really fine stained glass in Sussex churches is sadly limited; where it is not plain dull it is usually crude and garish.

Fittleworth sports three bridges, all close together at the lower end of the village. One is opposite a fine old water mill which has the date A.D. 1742 inscribed on its stonework. It had two wheels on the north and west faces of the mill; both are now in ruins, although a good bit of that on the west face remains. The mill building is in good order and one can walk across the wooden plank bridges to the mill and watch the water rushing down through the sluices underneath. On the south side is the mill pond, all silence and calm with willows touching the water. Beyond this is the Arun, which flows under Fittleworth's second bridge, and continues towards Hardham and the sea between high banks, built to prevent it flooding the low-lying meadows on either side. The third bridge, just before the road leaves the levels of the water meadows and climbs again through the trees towards the Downs and Arundel, is that over the old railway line. This is now a pleasant, if somewhat overgrown walk; Fittleworth station still exists, at least it did the last time I visited it, but it may well have collapsed since then for its wooden awning hung at a crazy angle apparently defying the laws of gravity, which it can hardly do for much longer.

The old railway line from Midhurst through Fittleworth connected with the main Horsham to Arundel line at Hardham; the presence of a junction at such a quiet spot brought it for a while into the affairs of the outside world, but Hardham possesses a much greater and more permanent claim to fame. Many Sussex churches possess small pieces of wall paintings and a few possess complete ones, often rather heavily restored, but there is nothing in the western part of the county, and practically nothing in the country, to match the paintings at St Botolph's, Hardham. They were done some time after 1100 and are so extensive as to virtually cover the walls of the small nave and chancel. They had been plastered over for many centuries and were only re-discovered 100 years ago. A few were lost before their significance was realized and others have not been as well preserved as they might, but for all that it is at least possible to make out the subject of almost every painting. The colours for the most part are shades of red and yellow ochre, although in places greens and blues can be distinguished. The best-preserved pictures are those on the west wall of the chancel which depict Adam and Eve receiving the apple from the snake, and those of various scenes in the life of St George on the north wall of the nave. These latter have great historical significance for they are the earliest known pictures of St George painted in England; he had been put to death some 100 years earlier.

The church itself is very simple, almost certainly Saxon, with thick walls and small windows. It is situated on what was the original main Pulborough to Arundel road but this has now been bypassed, leaving the church and the cottages beside it in a quiet lane. Old as the church is, it dates from no earlier than the middle period of Hardham's history for the village is first re-corded as being in existence in Roman times. Somewhere around A.D. 50 when Stane Street was being constructed to link Regnum with Londinium, Hardham was chosen for the site of a posting station. These occurred every 13 miles, Hardham being the first, Alfoldean, close to the Surrey border, being the second, and in all probability there were two more, at Dorking and Merton. A posting station was not unlike the type of fort depicted in films about the American West, consisting to a wooden rectangular enclosure with the road passing through the middle. A good deal of Roman material is incorporated in the walls of the church.

There was also an Augustine priory at Hardham, to the south of the church, and of this the roofless chapter house and the walls of the refectory—incorporated in a farmhouse—remain.

The hamlets of Coldwaltham and Watersfield follow Hardham in close succession and then the road swings southwards towards Bury. The line of Stane Street continues south-westwards to Bignor and the site of a Roman villa. Bignor is one of three small villages—the others are West Burton and Sutton—which lie on a narrow lane which winds along under the northern face of the Downs. All contain some lovely houses and cottages, mostly in flint, although there is some wood framing and brick, and many are thatched. West Burton is perhaps only a hamlet for it has no church, but the late sixteenth-century Coke's House and the walls and farm buildings are as fine an example of stone construction as any in the county. Sutton, although hardly any bigger than West Burton, does have a church, at the north end of the village, dating largely from the twelfth to fourteenth centuries. The Church of Holy Cross, Bignor, is built on the site of one mentioned in Domesday and the font, east wall of the nave and the chancel arch date from this time. The rest is thirteenth century, although much restored in eighteenth and nineteenth.

The Roman villa which is in a field at the east end of the village, was discovered by a farmer in 1811, whilst ploughing, although the existence of Roman remains had long been known. Part of the church is said to contain Roman building material and in 1740 elephant bones were found in the ground and it is known that the Romans used elephants at Regnum. The villa was first excavated in the 1820s and proved to be one of the largest known Roman houses in Britain, covering over four acres. The principal relics, apart from the basic outline of the building, are the very fine mosaics.

# 7

# From Haywards Heath to Heathfield

BALCOMBE could easily have become another Burgess Hill or Hassocks for it lies on both the main London to Brighton railway line and the busy B2036 Horley to Brighton road. There are a number of substantial Victorian villas along the main road and beside them stands the station from which it is possible to reach London Bridge in 46 minutes, yet Balcombe remains a small village deep in the much reduced but still extensive forest from which it takes its name.

The parish church of St Mary, up on a bank on the east side of the main road and almost hidden by trees, marks the real beginning of the village although there are outlying houses and shops some distance to the north. The oldest parts of St Mary's are Norman and there is some early seventeenth-century stained glass in the south window, but a good deal of it is heavy Victorian, a result of extensive restorations in 1847 and 1872. A good deal more elegant is a recent addition: three panels in a handwritten script hanging near the door, the Apostles' Creed, the Ten Commandments, and the Lord's Prayer. Beside the church is a white-boarded lodge to Balcombe House, the latter dating from 1760 and originally the parsonage house, whilst opposite is a rather superior sort of log cabin belonging to the 1st Balcombe Scouts. The crossroads at the centre of the village, east of the B2036, is approached by

way of a handsome, high wooden barn now used as a builders'
store, a large timber-frame house and a former coach house. On
two sides is a large, three-storey block of shops dating from the
early years of this century, opposite is Forge Cottage, name and
building both evocative of an earlier period in Balcombe's history,
whilst the fourth corner is occupied by the Half Moon public
house. Behind there are more houses and cottages, the cricket
field and a second entrance to Balcombe House, whilst beyond is
the forest. It is worth continuing out of the village in the direction
of Haywards Heath until one of the great structures of the railway age comes into view. The thirty-seven arches of the 1,475
foot long Balcombe Viaduct carry the London to Brighton line
across the valley of the River Ouse, now bearing much greater
weights and a far more intensive service than was ever envisaged
when it was erected in 1839–41, yet it has needed no special
strengthening and is just as it was built. The Ouse over which it
passes is little more than a stream, although at one time it was
broad enough to carry barges; almost the last occasion on which
it did so was when the bricks for the viaduct were brought up
from Lewes.

Lindfield, immediately north-east of Haywards Heath, has long
been regarded as one of the most picturesque of Sussex villages,
a status confirmed in 1934 when it was so voted by readers of the
*Sussex County Magazine*. Lindfield possesses what Pevsner declares
to be "without any doubt the finest village street in East Sussex",
a half-mile long collection of houses and cottages, with the
thirteenth-century church of St John the Baptist at one end and
the pond and the extensive green at the other. It is, in short, what
many people would regard as the typical English village and consequently receives many visitors. Lindfield was not always so pleasant a place and in the years immediately after the Napoleonic
Wars many of its inhabitants, like so many in Sussex, lived in
great poverty. In 1824 the Quaker William Allen settled at
Gravelye House in Lindfield, and on 100 acres on the south side
of West Common, bought by his friend John Smith, MP, of Dale

Park, he set up a number of smallholdings. These, complete with cottage and stock, he let out at a rent of 4s. per week. After a hesitant start the scheme became a great success and Allen went on to build a school, teaching workshops, a boarding school for poor children from Ireland and elsewhere, and a library. He and his wife taught some of the local people to read and a newspaper was produced. Allen's work attracted great attention and he worked tirelessly to improve the lot of the underprivileged far beyond Lindfield and Sussex. He was an associate of Wilberforce in his campaign to abolish slavery, a partner of Robert Owen the great socialist, and also a friend of the Duke of Sussex and the Czar of Russia. He twice visited Russia setting up settlements there, founded twenty schools in Greece, and worked for reform in Spain. This extraordinary man died in Lindfield in 1843, leaving the village vastly more prosperous than he had found it. A number of the dormitory buildings of Allen's British school survive, grouped around an enclosed garden called Pelham Place and facing the common.

Various small industries, piano-, candle-, paper- and glove-making, went on in Victorian times and stage coaches passed through Lindfield on their way from London to Brighton, but the railway age brought great changes to this part of Sussex. The nearest the railway came to Lindfield was Haywards Heath and it gradually took over Lindfield's role, whilst Lindfield became largely residential, populated by retired people and those who work in Brighton and London.

Cuckfield is almost large enough to be a town. In 1254 it was granted a charter, it has a hospital which serves a large part of the surrounding district, a main street with some twenty shops, and it might even be said to possess suburbs. Yet I think we may call it a village for it has the air of one and in contrast to Haywards Heath, which it adjoins and which has far outstripped it in size since the coming of the railway, it certainly looks like one. The focal point, as in many other Sussex villages, is the church, but it is especially so with Holy Trinity, Cuckfield. It is a fine church built mainly in the Perpendicular style, with a high steeple set above the tower and dominating the village. Holy Trinity lies at the southernmost point of Cuckfield with fields sloping gently away below it to give an unobscured view of the Downs eight miles distant. Around the church is a group of buildings reminiscent of the Causeway at Horsham on a much smaller scale, and beyond this the main road makes a right-angled turn on its way in from Bolney and Brighton and heads up the hill through the centre of the village towards Haywards Heath and Balcombe. It is a road Cuckfield, I am sure, would be happy to be without. It is hardly able to cope with the constant stream of lorries attempting to negotiate it. So wide and long are they and so narrow the street, that is it a wonder everything didn't coagulate into an inextricable tangle long ago. It is difficult enough for pedestrians to cross the road, but they can hardly consider themselves safe when they have gained the far pavement for lorry wheels are constantly scrubbing against the curb and encroaching upon it whilst their loads hang further over still. Despite the traffic Cuckfield has a lot to recommend it, with excellent shops, a handy situation for Brighton and the Downs, and some fine buildings. The church stands high above all, the lovely, deep, resonant chime of its clock sounding the hours as it has done since 1867. In that year, it re-placed a 200-year-old clock, now hanging on the north wall, which was made by a local blacksmith, Isaac Leney. One of the features of the church is its monuments, there being no less than thirteen to the Burrell family who were originally ironmasters, and who still live in Ockenden Manor, a partly sixteenth-century house situated in a lane under the shadow of the church. Then there is the elaborate and ornate memorial to Charles Sergison. He bought Cuckfield Park, an Elizabethan mansion set in ex-tensive grounds which adjoin the main road south of the village, and which remained in the family until a few years ago. Of more recent date is a memorial on the south wall to a Cuckfield resi-dent who was drowned in the *Lusitania* disaster, whilst the memorial to those who died in the two world wars is outside the church on the south side. When the church was restored in the mid-nineteenth century, C. E. Kempe, better known as a designer of stained-glass windows, was commissioned to paint the roof of the nave. The result is a powerful piece of decoration, typical of the mid-Victorian period, but free from the excessive opulence common a few years later.

Due south of Cuckfield is Burgess Hill, an area which is now very much larger than a village, having experienced two periods of tremendous growth, first in the 1930s, then in the 1960s. Wivelsfield Station lies within the Burgess Hill conglomeration—the railway being the principal reason for the village's expansion, providing easy access to London and Brighton—but Wivelsfield itself, to the east, lies outside. The oldest part of the parish church of St Peter and St John the Baptist dates from the eleventh century, although most of it is of thirteenth-, fourteenth- and fifteenth-century origin, rebuilt in the nineteenth. There are some large, handsome houses in the village and a very big green, the best part of a mile to the south-east.

Ditchling, south again, also has a green or common some distance from the village. Ditchling itself is a very attractive village, enhanced by a fine setting hard against the Downs. The Haywards Heath to Brighton and Lewes to Horsham roads meet in the narrow centre, just to the east of the largely thirteenth-century parish church of St Margaret. Opposite the church is the quite beautiful Anne of Cleves' house a pile of mellow red brick, timber frames, flint, barge boards and tiles which gives the impression it is a work of nature which has grown and spread like a Sussex oak rather than as a result of the efforts of man. Its name has led to all sorts of mis-statements. One alleged authority claims that the house "has nothing to do with" Anne of Cleves, whilst another insists that she lived in it as a "Much beloved lady of the manor". In the early 1900s, when part of it housed the village library, it was known as King Alfred's Palace and a local inhabitant said no one in those days knew of any association with Anne. It is generally assumed that she did at one time own the house, even if she never lived in it, but this too is only supposition. The most reliable authority, undoubtedly, is the Sussex Archaeological Society, and I quote part of a letter from them on the subject.

T. W. Horsefield in his 'History of Antiquities of Lewes' page 245, lists the two Manors of Southover and Ditchling as belonging to the Priory. Anne of Cleves was granted the possession of Lewes Priory but it appears that there is no evidence that the house in Ditchling was part of the Manor property and there were several manors at Ditchling, any of which may have been the relevant one.

So the mystery remains; perhaps someone will one day discover an old document which will solve it.

Ditchling has long been a thriving cultural centre. In the 1920s the St Dominic's Press was founded by H. D. C. Pepper and a number of books of local interest were published, including an old Sussex miming play 'King George and the Turkish Knight'. The Press also produced three books by Eric Gill, who lived for a time in the village, as did his friend, the painter Frank Brangwyn. The Ditchling Players were a particularly well-known group of amateur actors who performed as far afield as Brighton and London. In addition to all this, weaving, spinning, pottery, jewellery, metal- and leather-working and etching were carried on in the village and an arts market was held twice a year. How all this would have been affected by a scheme mooted in 1939 to turn Ditchling into a garden city, with a five-fold increase in population, is a matter for conjecture, but the outbreak of war ensured the scheme's demise. Ditchling remains a village more concerned than most with the arts; its most famous resident is Vera Lynn.

Immediately above the village is the 813-foot Ditchling Beacon, the third highest point on the South Downs and very possibly the most visited one of all. The road from the village leads up to it and continues on over the Downs past the racecourse and into Brighton, whilst an even more precipitous route is the Nye, an ancient Celtic trackway which may still be followed by walkers.

Hamsey, Offham and Cooksbridge are a group of hamlets east of Ditchling and north of Lewes, which together make one parish and thus, it might be argued a village. Hamsey certainly was a village as far back as 925 when King Athelstan held a meeting of his counsellors there, and it is mentioned as a manor in Domesday. The manor house stood on the site of the present churchyard, and the church goes back to the days when Hamsey was a place of some importance. It was abandoned in 1860 when a new church was erected at Offham, but since the 1920s a good deal of effort has gone into its restoration and upkeep and it is still sometimes used for services. No one seems to know just why Hamsey declined, although it is believed locally that it was as a result of an outbreak of plague.

The second most important battle in Sussex history was fought on the Downs up above Offham on 14 May 1264 when Simon de Montfort defeated Henry III and established the first steps towards democracy. Simon's army camped in and around Offham the night before and many died here when they were overwhelmed by Prince Edward's cavalry early next morning before the battle turned in Simon's favour. To the west, at Plumpton, the King's men died by the hundreds later in the day, and when the railway which runs through Plumpton and Cooksbridge to Lewes was being constructed in 1845 no less than fifteen wagonloads of bones were unearthed. In terms of casualties in relation to the number of men who took part, the Battle of Lewes was one of the bloodiest of all time, and bones and fragments of weapons are still ploughed up from time to time.

Barcombe, immediately north of Cooksbridge, is a large parish bisected by the Ouse and embracing Barcombe village, Barcombe Mills, Barcombe Cross and Spithurst. It is lush, low-lying countryside with many fine houses, the parish church of St Mary with its typically Sussex shingled broach spire occupying perhaps the best setting of all, a lovely view to the south across the water meadows to Lewes and the Caburn. Barcombe Mills has a most aptly named pub, the 'Anglers Rest', beside the abandoned railway station and close to the river. It is a favourite with fishermen who frequent the banks of the Ouse hereabouts. The area is subject to severe flooding and there are a number of road signs permanently in position ready to warn motorists and walkers of the dangers; there is also a curious sign beside the level crossing informing the public that they may use railway property when all other means of access are blocked.

The parish news, edited by the Rector, is unusually ecumenical in that it lists not only services and events associated with the parish church and St Francis, Barcombe Cross, and St Bartholomew, Spithurst, but also records the addresses of the Providence Baptist Chapel, Barcombe Evangelical Free Church and St Pancras Roman Catholic Church, Lewes. It is a real local newspaper, with a monthly recipe, bowls club results, and news from all the village organizations and is distributed free to "every household in the village".

Chailey is an even larger parish than Barcombe. A great deal could be and has been written about the charitable works performed by Chailey people and we have space only to consider two. In 1903 two social workers from Bermondsey, Mrs Kimmins and Miss Rennie, rented a house in Station Road, Chailey, as a nursing home for boys from the East End who were suffering from tuberculosis. In a little while they moved into the old workhouse, which was in a deplorable state with leaking roofs, no gas or electricity and overrun with rats, and from this has grown the institution known throughout Britain as Chailey Heritage. Today it occupies three main sites around Chailey Common at the northern end of the village. The Heritage cares for over 200 physically handicapped children whose ages range from a few weeks to sixteen years. It is administered by the Ministry of Health and costs half a million pounds to run each year; when Mrs Kimmins and Miss Rennie moved into the old workhouse in 1903 their funds stood at £5. The Heritage is perhaps best known for its work with thalidomide children, but today nearly half its patients suffer from spina bifida. The children it deals with are far more severely handicapped than were those original TB sufferers, severe though this illness could be; a number are illegitimate and some have mental problems as well. Many prominent people have given help and encouragement to the marvellous work done by the Heritage, including the Queen, the Queen Mother and Princess Margaret. In 1936 they visited Chailey to open the Silver Jubilee Building for Toddlers and the Duchess of York, as she then was, promised that when her daughters were old enough to take up public duties on their own the Heritage would be the first place they would visit. She kept her word and in 1945 all three returned to Chailey, the occasion being marked by a promise of £50,000 from Sir Henry and Lady Price of Wakehurst Place, Ardingly, towards more extensions. In 1963 Princess Margaret returned again, to open the Experimental Workshop, financed by the Lady Hoare Thalidomide Appeal Fund.

Rather less well known than the Heritage is Father Basil Jellicoe, an Anglo-Catholic priest who was born in Chailey in 1899, the son of the Rector. From 1922 to 1927 he was head of Magdalen College Mission to Somers Town and Curate of St Mary's church there. Somers Town lies immediately north of St Pancras and in the 1920s was an area where the most dreadful poverty was commonplace. Father Jellicoe devoted himself to alleviating the lot of the unfortunate people who lived there and to hastening slum clearance. He wore himself out and had to convalesce back in Sussex. Here he noted that poverty, whilst not on the scale of that in the great cities and not so easily detectable, existed to a considerable degree amongst farm labourers and the unemployed in the country and their families, and in 1934 he set up the St Richard Housing Association. Its first homes were at Portslade and Midhurst and soon others followed at Pulborough, Flimwell, Harting and elsewhere. After speaking at an association meeting at Pulborough in July 1935, Father Jellicoe, much weakened by his efforts on behalf of the underprivileged wherever he found them, collapsed and within a month he was dead. He was not yet thirty-seven. In the words of the Archbishop of York,

Steam-train revival at Horsted Keynes

The village green at Lindfield

Waiting for the bus, West Hoathly

Thomas Turner's house, East Hoathly

Chiddingly church seen from the Tudor barn

The Hellingly donkeys

Thomas Dallaway's mill at Blackdown, Punnett's Town

The village pond at Wisborough Green

The lead font at Pyecombe

The Ouse at Piddinghoe

The Long Man of Wilmington, seen from the end of the village street

"Basil Jellicoe was one of Christ's most precious gifts to the Church of our generation".

Chailey Common—more accurately the North Common— around which the Heritage buildings stand, is one of the largest commons in Sussex and is carefully watched over by the Chailey Commons Society, formed in 1964 and now with over 300 members. One of the buildings now owned by the Heritage is the windmill which is said to stand at the dead centre of Sussex. The village centre lies on the Lewes road, south of the common. There is a small green beside the much restored parish church of St Peter; the buildings around it are residential although a number were at one time shops.

In the north-east corner of the parish of Chailey is Sheffield Park, known to many visitors for its magnificent rhododendron gardens, owned by the National Trust, and the Bluebell Railway, first of all the preserved standard gauge steam lines. It began in 1960 when a group of enthusiasts bought from British Railways a Terrier tank engine of the former London, Brighton and South Coast Railway and a former Southern Railway corridor coach. Now there are dozens of locomotives, including two Terriers, one in its original gorgeous mustard colour, and a somewhat later and larger Brighton tank engine named Birch Grove after the nearby house belonging to Mr Harold Macmillan. Many of the carriages were once owned by the Southern Railway and have been restored to the green livery which was so familiar on the Sussex lines until a few years back. The Bluebell Railway has plans to reopen the long section of line from Horsted Keynes through to West Hoathly and East Grinstead and thus reconnect itself with British Rail.

Horsted Keynes is the present terminus of the line. The village itself is a mile away—one of the reasons why British Railways could never make the line pay—a wooded place set on a Wealden ridge.

Ardingly, once the intermediate station between Horsted Keynes and Haywards Heath, is a village chiefly notable for the extensive grounds of the South of England Show and as the one-time home

H

of Frances Wolseley. The South of England Show takes place each June and attracts enormous crowds, transforming the normally quiet village. Everyone who is anyone in the agricultural, horticultural and horse worlds attends and it is one of the social events of the year.

Ardingly's most famous resident, Viscountess Wolseley, lived at Culpepers, a house near the village she designed for herself. Culpeper is the name of a family which built Wakehurst Place, one mile to the north of the village, in 1590. There are memorial brasses to members of the family in the parish church of St Peter, and the house now belongs to the National Trust. It has been let to the Ministry of Agriculture who have created what has become known as "Little Kew". It comprises four acres of water gardens where rare marsh plants in danger of extinction are cultivated. At the opposite end of the village, where the roads from Haywards Heath and Lindfield join, is the village sign. On one side are the arms of the Culpeper family and on the other those of Viscountess Wolseley, the latter in a framework of wheat-ears, hops and other symbols representing Frances Wolseley's interest in things of the countryside. The sign was erected by the Sussex Archaeological Trust as a memorial to her. She died in 1937, leaving behind a great store of knowledge of Sussex. All her records, documents, etc. were bequeathed to Hove Public Library. She had published 111 articles in the *Sussex County Magazine* on historic houses in the county; others were completed or almost so and appeared after her death. The daughter of Sir Garnet Wolseley, the great reformer of the British army, she was born in Dublin in 1872. In her youth she knew Lord Tennyson and John Sargent. When she first came to Sussex she lived at Glynde, and in 1925 she moved to her own house at Ardingly. By all accounts, Frances Wolseley, a viscountess in her own right, was not only a great source of knowledge of all things to do with Sussex, but also a friend of many Sussex people, especially the policemen, the roadmenders, gardeners and others with whom she came into contact in Ardingly.

It was a sad coincidence that another well-known writer on

Sussex, George Forrester Scott, who wrote under the pseudonym John Hailsham, should also die in Ardingly in 1937. Of his books *Idehurst*, which was about Lindfield, and *Lonewood Corner*, set in Ardingly, the editor of the *Sussex County Magazine* wrote: "I know no Sussex books that convey so perfectly to the reader the sense of the Wealden Landscape, and the characters of the old Sussex peasants."

The most interesting part of West Hoathly lies off the main road and is therefore easily missed. West Hoathly stands all but 600 feet up on a ridge on the westernmost tip of the Ashdown Forest astride the Wych Cross to Turners Hill Road. One may look both north and south and see a landscape given over to woods and forests. The main street runs south from this road, rising at first and then dipping down to the village centre around which stands the church of St Margaret, the Old Parsonage and the Cat Inn. Beside the lych gate is a rubbish bin presented by the *East Grinstead Courier* in 1960 to mark West Hoathly's achieving second place in the best-kept village competition. The view from here southwards where the churchyard dips down is particularly fine. This was once iron country and there are some cast-iron tomb slabs inside the church and iron furnishings around the fireplace of the Cat Inn, all of local origin.

A mile to the north is the Elizabethan manor house of Gravetye whose first owner was Richard Infield, an ironmaster. In the early years of the present century Gravetye became famous when the owner, William Robinson, who was a well-known landscape gardener, laid out the gardens in a manner which was extensively copied. Amongst the buildings clustered around the church are the fifteenth-century timber-framed Priest's House which now belongs to the Sussex Archaeological Society and a charming stone bus shelter erected by Godwin and Charlotte King in 1948. Next to it, on the wall of the Old Parsonage, is a plaque affixed in the Coronation Year of 1953 to mark the ownership of the manor by the first Queen Elizabeth in 1558. The church of St Margaret goes back at least to the thirteenth century; it is a handsome building, protected by an unusually heavy oak door, with some nice stained glass over the altar and an old seventeenth-century clock which was working until recently but has now been retired for it was in need of repairs which would have destroyed its character.

West Hoathly is one of a group of villages and hamlets lying on or just beyond the southern fringes of the Ashdown Forest. In the Middle Ages the forest was a deer preserve of John of Gaunt and the 14,000 acres were fenced in, although from the earliest times the farmers living around it had grazing rights, whilst on the northern slopes the iron industry flourished. There has always been conflict which continues to this day between the various parties who had access or wished to have access to the forest, but it remains an extensive and at times desolate expanse of heathland and forest. The deer are still there, although they are not often seen near the roads.

Nutley marks the southern edge of the forest and is where northbound traffic on the A22 enters it, dipping down before climbing up through the open heath, levelling off where it enters the trees, then finally descending again past the junction with the A275 Lewes and Newhaven Road at Wych Cross towards Forest Row. Nutley is an unassuming place, a mixture of fairly old and relatively new, its only notable feature a restored windmill on the Crowborough Road. Due east of it, on the A275, is Danehill, a pretty little village set on high ground with, like Nutley, a Victorian parish church.

Maresfield is a large village, adjoining Nutley on the A22, with an army camp on its western outskirts. The parish church of St Bartholomew, a handsome building incorporating some original Norman windows and doorways, overlooks the crossroads in the centre of Maresfield and the abrupt right-angle turn the narrow A22 makes beside the churchyard wall. South of it is the green, whilst on the north side are the gates to the largely demolished Maresfield Park. Piltdown Common, of Piltdown Man fame, is a mile to the west along the A272 Winchester Road, within the parish of Maresfield.

Beyond is Newick, a village with a good selection of handsome houses and cottages and a carefully restored church, St Mary's, with a Perpendicular sandstone tower. The Bull Inn, beside the Green, is named after the papal bull or seal, a reminder that Newick lies on the Pilgrims' Way from Winchester to Canterbury. The modern A272 follows this route for a good part of its way and there is a signpost showing the distance to Winchester in the village.

To the east of Maresfield, on the A272, is Buxted, a village with particularly strong links with the iron industry. In 1543 the first iron cannon in the country was cast here by a Frenchman, Peter Baude, and two local men, Ralph Hogge and William Levett, the latter being Rector of Buxted. Ernest Straker, in his definitive book on the subject, *Wealden Iron*, describes the three as "the fathers of the Wealden Cannon-founding industry". Hogge had a house built in the village in 1581 with a cast-iron slab over the doorway bearing the figure of a hog and the date. It stands today, by the entrance to Buxted Park, on the A272 west of the village. The parish church of Buxted is in the grounds of Buxted Park, a house dating from 1726 which once belonged to the Earl of Liverpool. Of late it has been put to various uses; for a time it was a health farm, patronized by a number of celebrities including the well-known Sussex character Rosie Meades. The southern edge of Buxted Park adjoins one of the many estates erected in Uckfield during the last decade.

In the quiet, flat countryside within the triangle bounded by Uckfield, Lewes and Hailsham are a number of hamlets and small villages which, whilst not really remote, remain undisturbed and not greatly affected by the twentieth century.

Most of the houses in Isfield, three miles south-west of Uckfield, are grouped between the river and the station, the latter having closed in 1970. This event took a number of people by surprise, including, it would seem, British Rail, who had plans ready for re-routing the line into Lewes to facilitate the building of a new road bridge. Trains still reach Uckfield, from Tunbridge Wells and

London, but the missing section through Isfield and Barcombe Mills means that the valuable alternative route between London and the Sussex coast has been breached and there is continuing agitation for it to be restored. Isfield and Barcombe Mills are both haunts of anglers. They have the river all to themselves now, apart from the wild life which makes a home on or around it, but once it was navigable and for a while carried a good deal of commercial traffic. The last barge reached Isfield in 1868, but pleasure craft beat their way through the weeds and undergrowth for another ten years.

Halland and East Hoathly are adjacent villages on the A22 between Uckfield and Hailsham, neither grown very large on account of it, although Halland has a motel and East Hoathly a few new houses. The road through the latter makes a sudden 90-degree turn, as at Maresfield, bringing motorists down to a speed at which they are able to read a plaque attached to a pleasant red-brick house on the north side of the road. It commemorates Thomas Turner who lived in the house and who kept a diary which since its publication many years after his death has become something of a classic and is recognized as providing some of the most entertaining and revealing insights of village life in the eighteenth century.

Ringmer is four miles south-west of Halland on the B2192 and barely two miles from Lewes. Its finest feature is its green, a meeting and recreational place for everyone in the middle of the village and only a mile from the Downs. The village sign, which stands on the green by the turning for the church, commemorates two local women who married famous men associated with America —Ann Sadler, the wife of the founder of Harvard, and Gulielma Springett, wife of William Penn. Gulielma was born after the death of her father Sir William Springett who died at the siege of Arundel during the Civil War. The much restored and very carefully maintained church of St Mary the Virgin dates originally from Norman times. Ringmer sees many visitors when the Glyndebourne operas are being held, just over the hill. Laughton, three miles east of Ringmer on the Lewes to Hailsham road, although of no great size, nevertheless has its own written history, copies of which could be obtained, so the *Sussex County Magazine* reported in 1934, "from the postmaster". There was obviously a great upsurge of community feeling around that time for in both 1927 and 1929 pageants written by the vicar were staged at Laughton illustrating episodes in Sussex history. That in the latter year was held to mark the founding of the parish church of All Saints in 1229 and ninety people took part. The small collection of buildings which make up the village form a pleasing group on a bend in the main road, the church being down a lane, whilst further south again is a red and black brick tower, the ruins of Laughton Place, one of the homes of the famous Sussex family of Pelham. It was abandoned in favour of a mansion at Halland which in its turn was given up; the remains of this are incorporated in Halland Park Farm. The Vicar of Laughton lives at Chiddingly, some three miles north-east of Laughton across the A22, and in the church there are relics of the Pelhams, although more prominent are those of the Jefferay family. The Jefferays lived at Chiddingly Place, one more abandoned mansion now incorporated into a farmhouse. It says something for the impermanence of position and property that the cottages and the humble families subject to the wills and pleasures of the great families survive, whilst the great families and their mansions are either gone or much reduced. The spire of the parish church of Chiddingly is 128 feet high and is one of the only five stone spires in the county.

Chiddingly lies in the midst of a maze of narrow lanes and is consequently one of the quietest and least visited villages in Sussex; I had driven within a couple of miles of it literally hundreds of times before I ever went there. When I did the stillness was almost eerie, and certainly the neglected, although not abandoned, atmosphere of Chiddingly Place with the huge Tudor barn beside it, once a wing of the house and with the filled-in windows dating from those days prominent, was oppressively powerful.

Upper Dicker, Ripe and Chalvington, due west of Hailsham,

are hardly villages, the former though is well known as the one-
time home of Horatio Bottomley, pioneer of the popular weekly
magazine and larger-than-life benefactor or villain according to
one's point of view. Arlington, nearby, again is really only a hamlet but it has a fine Norman flint church, a stock-car racing circuit
which makes a great deal of noise and provides a lot of entertainment, and a reservoir where I once came across an Irishman, who
had previously been employed as a footman at Buckingham Palace,
painting the bridge.

Horsebridge is practically a suburb of Hailsham. It possesses a
flour mill which as I write has been up for sale for a considerable
time and is now in a sadly derelict state. There are a few shops
and low-lying fields which are frequently flooded when the Cuckmere overflows. To the north is Hellingly. Although within twenty
minutes' walk of the rapidly expanding town of Hailsham and
possessed of one of the largest mental hospitals in the country, it
remains a small, compact village where one is as likely to encounter
pedestrians as cars on the lanes which pass through it. In the dead
centre of Hellingly is the parish church of St Peter and Paul.

In pre-Christian days burial grounds were always remote from
the settlements to which they were attached. This remained the
case in the Celtic and Roman eras, but subsequently superstitions
grew less strong and around A.D. 750 the church regularized what
was already becoming accepted practice and allowed burial grounds
beside the church and within the village. But the point had not
yet been reached when it was permitted to build the church
actually within the traditional burial ground or barrow and this
did not occur until the century after the Norman Conquest when
church building was proceeding at such a rate that the old taboo
began to break down. Hellingly is typical of a village church built
within the ancient, pre-Christian, burial ground, but nowhere else
in Sussex is it possible to see so clearly the shape of the barrow
with the church in its middle and the houses all around. The four
original gates remain, on three sides there is a wall, in parts six
to seven feet high, marking the raised barrow, whilst on the fourth

side the houses are separated from the churchyard only by a path.

St Peter and Paul is a handsome church with solid, heavy pews recently restored to their natural colour which has done much to lighten the interior, an uncomfortably florid-looking Victorian organ, and a chancel noticeably askew in relation to the nave. There are a number of theories to account for this, one of the least likely being the alleged inability of the Norman builders to keep a straight line—which they obviously could—one of the more probable being that it represents the inclination of the Saviour's head hanging from the cross.

All of the houses and cottages around the church, in their various ways, complement it. On the north-east corner is a paddock inhabited by a pair of donkeys and a little way down the road a thirteenth-century water mill stands beside the Cuckmere. Further on, under a disused railway bridge, there are signs of industry: on the left waste ground once occupied by a plant-hire firm, on the right nurseries and a road haulage contractor's yard. At the end of this road is the entrance to Hellingly Hospital. The hospital consists of a collection of buildings dominated by an ugly Victorian brick tower but set in extensive and beautifully kept gardens.

To the south-east of the church is a pub, the Golden Martlet, the station, now a private residence where washing may be seen strung between the awning supports on the platform, and, set in a field next to it, Horselunges Manor. This latter, very carefully restored in 1925, is considered to be one of the finest large timber-framed houses in Sussex. It dates from either the late fifteenth or early sixteenth century.

East of the Hellingly–Heathfield A267 road and west of Battle there are a number of what are really large hamlets rather than villages—Cowbeech, Rushlake Green, Warbleton, Ponts Green, Bodle Street Green and Penhurst—in the lush, undulating Wealden countryside immediately north of the Pevensey Marshes, but the next village proper is Horam, north of Hellingly on the A267. It is

the home of a flourishing and—for England—rare industry, that
of wine-making. The Merrydown Company is probably best known
for its cider but it also makes  great quantities of wine, most of
which is exported. Many people make their own wine, of course,
but to find a firm successfully selling its own English wine is un-
common. The head office is situated in the old manor house. Much
of Horam, including the parish church of Christ Church, which
was built in 1890, dates from Victorian times or later and grew
up around the now abandoned railway station. Incidentally the
next station up the line, Heathfield, was for many years lit by
natural gas which was found in small quantities locally.

Heathfield is not a very large town yet it manages to cover a
great area and the ribbon development of the 1920s and '30s has
meant that it is well on the way to absorbing a number of adjoining villages and hamlets, including Cross-in-Hand, Cade Street,
Broadoak and Punnett's Town. The latter possesses a rather remarkable windmill, Blackdown, and one evening in June I visited it. I
had often seen it standing on the ridge east of Heathfield but this
particular evening it made an unusually arresting sight, its brilliant white weather-boarded sides standing out against the deep
blue sky. As I drew nearer, from the direction of Cowbeech, I
realized the sweeps were turning; I negotiated a series of steep,
narrow lanes and arrived to find a man in late middle age with a
weatherbeaten face standing at the doorway. "Is this your mill?"
I asked, and he replied, "It is, and my father's before me, and his
father's before him." He went on to tell me that he had lived beside it since 1914, that it had ceased active work in the late 1920s,
and he had spent "half my life" restoring it.

Later I investigated the mill's history in the library at Brighton
and found that its owner, William Dallaway, had modestly told
only a part of his family's involvement with it. It was erected by
Stephen Neve of Rushlake Green, two miles south of Punnett's
Town, in 1856, having been brought by cart from its original site
at Sissinghurst, Kent, by Daniel Hobden, the great uncle of William
Dallaway. The mill it replaced at Blackdown had been burnt and

this had been owned by the Dallaways since the end of the eighteenth century; one wonders if any other mill in the country has been in one family's ownership for so long. Blackdown Mill ceased to work in 1928 when the curb wore out, and six years later the cap was removed. By 1947 it was no more than an empty tower, used for storing cattle feed. It had by then passed into the ownership of Demas Dallaway, and his son William decided in that year to restore the mill to working order. Most restorations begin with a more or less whole structure but William Dallaway had nothing but an empty shell. However he persevered; a wind shaft was acquired from Staplecross and slowly the mill came back to life. The work is almost done now and Blackdown Mill stands as a unique monument to one man's dedication.

# 8

# *The South Downs and East towards Rye*

PYECOMBE, although small, is one of the most distinguished of Sussex villages for it provides what is probably the strongest living link between the present time and the days when the county was the centre of Britain's iron industry. Before the Industrial Revolution a good deal of the products of the Sussex ironmakers was for agricultural use, and from at least as early as the sixteenth century shepherds' crooks have been made in the county. In the forge at Pyecombe the blacksmith, Scotsman Sean Black, still manufactures crooks for shepherds on the South Downs and elsewhere, some going as far afield as New Zealand and Australia. The previous blacksmith, George Mitchell, whose father was also a Pyecombe blacksmith and worked until the age of ninety-five, died in 1956 and it looked as if the industry would die with him, but fortunately Sean Black discovered and revived it. The forges at Kingston-on-Lewes and Falmer, both close by, were also well known for their crooks but Pyecombe is the most famous of all.

The village is situated at one of the busiest intersections in Sussex where the A273 Haywards Heath and Burgess Hill and the A23 London roads converge to run through the Downs into Brighton. There is a pub and a garage and a collection of caravans by the junction but on the hill above the noise of the traffic fades to a muted purr and the small flintstone church and the houses—

which include a converted chapel—and cottages around it stand undisturbed amongst the sheep-covered hillsides. The gate to the churchyard is unusual in that it is pivoted in the middle and is known as a Tapsell gate. There are similar ones at East Dean, Friston, Jevington and Kingston, but hardly any outside East Sussex. It is assumed that they take their name from a Tapsell who was an ironmaster at Wadhurst. Even rarer is the font inside the church which is made of lead; there are only two others in Sussex, at Edburton and Parham. There were many more until the Civil War when they were used by Puritan troops to make bullets and there is a local tradition that the parishioners of Pyecombe whitewashed theirs to disguise it, hence the flecks of white still visible.

To the north-east of the crossroads by Pyecombe church stands a windmill on the summit of the Downs. It is one of the famous Clayton pair, known as Jack and Jill. Clayton village is even smaller than Pyecombe. It is a mile away, under the north face of the Downs, and consists of little more than a railway tunnel, a church, a farm, a handful of cottages and the mills. The tunnel was the scene of a bad accident back in 1861 when signalling was rudimentary and the chief method of keeping one train from running into the back of another was time and a sometimes misplaced faith in Providence. One hot August evening, when Brighton had been full of day-trippers, three trains left for London in close succession. The first ran out of steam in the tunnel, the second stopped behind it and started to back out and was run into by the third. Twenty-three people were killed.

Clayton has a history which goes back 3,000 years. Relics of Bronze Age burials have been found within the parish, the Roman road from Croydon to Portslade passed through Clayton and Roman tiled pavements have been discovered. The church of St John dates back to before the Conquest and on its walls are paintings where are estimated to be almost as old as the church itself and have made Clayton known far and wide. Some ten years ago an extensive programme of preservation was carried out revealing, in particular, a magnificent representation of the Last Judgement over the chancel arch. The amount of detail is staggering, especially as it in no way detracts from the overall sense of power conveyed by the entire series of pictures. They are no mere decoration but an integral part of the religious expression of the building. If they are typical of what was to be found in English country churches in medieval times then it is no wonder that ordinary people were such devout Christians for one could hardly fail to be inspired by such intense illustrations of faith.

Stanmer lies in the Downs, three miles south-east of Clayton if one cares to walk but almost twice this distance by road for it can only be approached from the south by a turning off the A27 Brighton to Lewes road through Stanmer Park. The park, the house and the village all belonged to the Pelhams, Earls of Chichester, until 1947 when they were bought by Brighton Corporation. The glorious park, less than four miles from the Palace Pier, is preserved—at least for the moment—as an open space for the people of Brighton, the gardens of the house are used as a nursery by the Parks and Gardens Department, and the house itself belongs to the University of Sussex. The University was built in the north-east corner of Stanmer Park in 1961, skilfully placed to blend in amongst the trees with the landscape, and it is not this but the proposed new ring road which threatens the Park. The Stanmer Preservation Society was founded in 1971 and one may hope that its efforts, combined with the fortuitous—in this instance—cuts in public expenditure may defeat the proposals. The Society has set up a museum in the grounds of the house, the principal exhibit of which is a horse gin, probably of seventeenth-century origin, for drawing water from a deep well. The excellent restoration of the gin was carried out by the Conservation Department of Brighton Corporation. Stanmer was designated a Conservation Area by the Corporation in 1970.

Stanmer village consists of little more than a single street which tapers away into a track over the Downs, fronted by a handful of cottages, one shop, a very long barn with pink painted weather-boarded sides and flintstone ends, and the church. This latter is an almost complete nineteenth-century reconstruction of a fourteenth-century one and is full of Pelham family memorials including those of the 6th and 7th Earls who died within eight days of each other in November 1926, the father aged fifty-five, the son aged twenty-one, the latter having contracted the former's fatal influenza. The 8th Earl, the younger brother of the 7th, also died young, killed at the age of thirty-two during World War II.

Across the main road from Stanmer is Falmer. The villages have many links and the station for the University is at Falmer. There was an accident on the line near here in 1851 when a train was derailed and five people were killed. It was alleged that a shepherd boy living in a house beside the railway had been playing on the line and left a plank of wood across it, but although given a most gruelling interrogation the boy maintained his innocence. For all that, a year later to the day the unfortunate lad was struck by lightning and killed and his guilt in the eyes of many of the superstitious country people thus confirmed. Falmer has the disadvantage of being situated at a point where the main road narrows on the brow of a hill and at a junction and is thus beset with traffic hazards, but if one can avoid these one may notice the dew pond surrounded by some quaint old cottages and the nineteenth-century church of St Lawrence. At one time there seemed to be a real danger of ribbon development extending both east and west from Falmer along the A27 and thus creating a built-up area linking Brighton with Lewes, but although there is little enough open country before Brighton begins, the designation of 400 acres along the road between Falmer and Lewes as part of the Downs Preservation Scheme has prevented any further encroachment.

The road from Falmer over the Downs descends through Woodingdean and Ovingdean, both Brighton suburbs, to Rottingdean and the sea. It might be argued that Rottingdean is also a suburb, but despite the development along the seafront it has preserved a village-like quality. It has had its moments, the most dramatic being in 1377 when the French attacked it, set it alight and killed many of the villagers. It was a great place for smuggling, an activity pursued with enthusiasm until surprisingly recent times as may be gauged by a one-time pupil-teacher in the village school at Falmer who recalled in an article in the *Sussex County Magazine* in 1929 being shown by the parish clerk a scar on his shoulder, the relic of a sword cut received from a preventative man when he was surprised whilst carrying brandy kegs up from Rottingdean.

Rottingdean was a great favourite in Victorian times with those who liked to live near, but not in, Brighton and has had some famous residents. There was Kipling, Burne Jones and William Nicholson, the latter living in the Grange, a lovely eighteenth-century house which had once been a school, numbering amongst its pupils Cardinal Manning and Lord Lytton. The Grange stands beside the village green and pond, in the company of other handsome houses and below the part Norman, part Early English flintstone church of St Margaret. Artists and architects of the recent past have left their mark on Rottingdean, Lutyens having added to the Grange, Burne Jones and William Morris designing stained-glass windows for the church, whilst most familiar of all is the once very *avant-garde*-looking but now somewhat dated St Dunstan's Home for the Blind of 1937–9 standing dramatically on the Downs immediately to the west of the village.

From Rottingdean the coast road ascends steeply to continue along the cliff top through Saltdean and Peacehaven, possibly the most reviled area of development along the whole south coast. Certainly it is hard to think of a less visually uplifting stretch of coastline, but ugliness is something one can live with if it has compensations and in Saltdean and Peacehaven it obviously has, for homes there are eagerly sought after and property values have always been high. There is a telling, if unflattering, description of a villa somewhere along this part of the coastline in Graham Greene's *Brighton Rock*. Peacehaven once produced a Miss Great Britain who, when asked by Michael Aspel if her home was as attractive as its name implied, loyally if not entirely objectively replied that it was.

However much the building-over of the land along the clifftop may be regretted, it no doubt largely accounts for the unspoilt state of the villages in the immediate hinterland. Telscombe Cliffs is part of the Saltdean/Peacehaven sprawl but Telscombe village, little more than a mile to the north, is as small, as carefully preserved and seemingly as remote as any village in the county. It owes its remoteness to the absence of any road linking it with the main coast one; all there is, is a track across the Downs for walkers. To reach the village by road one has to take the A275 linking Lewes and Newhaven and turn off at Southease up a lane which climbs the side of the Downs, affording splendid views across the Ouse valley to the tall chimney of the lime works at Beddingham with its plume of white smoke, and Firle Beacon beyond. Telscombe lies in a dip amongst an oasis of trees encompassed about by the bare hills, a village of flintstone houses, cottages and barns and a Norman church with the darkest interior I have ever come across.

Telscombe belongs to the same parish as Piddinghoe, although one has to pass through Southease to get from one to the other. Southease lies within a few hundred yards of the Ouse, Piddinghoe upon it, and each has a church with a round, twelfth-century flint tower; so also does St Michael's in Lewes. There are two schools of thought as to how these towers came to be erected. One is that it was simply easier to build a round shape with round flintstones, but this would hardly explain why every other twelfth-century flint tower in Sussex is either square or rectangular. The other explanation, and for my money the most likely, is that they were watchtowers from which a lookout could be kept for invaders. The first mention of Southease is in 966 when, together with Telscombe and South Heighton on the east bank of the river, it was granted by King Edgar to Hyde Abbey at Winchester. The watchtower, if such it was, would certainly have fulfilled its function in 1377 for the French sailed up the Ouse and a battle took place on its banks by Lewes, although there is no positive record that Southease was attacked.

I

Domesday notes that the village was a great place for herring fishing. The river was wider than it is now and probably came closer to Southease; in one year 38,500 herring were caught, against the 16,000 at Iford, 1½ miles upstream, and the 4,000 at Rodmell (between Southease and Iford) and Brighton. The A275 bypasses all four riverside villages, Iford, Rodmell, Southease and Piddinghoe, and thus all remain small and compact. Since 1944 the parishes of Rodmell and Southease have been combined; they also share a railway station on the Lewes to Newhaven and Seaford line which runs along the east bank of the Ouse. At Southease the road continues past the church and the Green to cross the only bridge over the Ouse between Lewes and Newhaven, whilst Rodmell lies on a road which comes to a dead end. St Peter's Church, Rodmell, is almost entirely Norman, although restored in Victorian times, and has a Sussex ironstone weather-vane. Virginia Woolf died while living in a house close by the church in 1941.

Iford, like Rodmell, lies on a tributary rather than on the Ouse itself and the church again is Norman, this time with much less evidence of nineteenth-century restoration. A mile or so North, west of the A275, is Kingston near Lewes. It lies hard against Kingston Hill, which is 586 feet above sea level. Juggs Arms at Kingston commemorates a Brighton fisherman who answered to that name and who for many years walked along the hilltop on his way to sell fish at Lewes. The fourteenth-century parish church is dedicated to the child martyr St Pancras, as was the great priory at Lewes. This latter was founded in 1077 by the Cluny Order and was its chief house in England. Immediately prior to the Battle of Lewes, Henry III took refuge in it. After the Dissolution it was almost totally demolished, much of the material finding a variety of uses in the neighbourhood of Lewes, and in and around the Manor House at Kingston are fragments from the priory.

A notice by the church door at Piddinghoe reads "The view from the north side is worth the detour", which it certainly is for one looks through the branches of the churchyard trees across the flats with yachts and other boats resting on them, over the broad sweep of the river to Southease and the Downs on either side of Lewes. Piddinghoe is very aware of its attractions and of its nautical associations—the first four cottages on the main street as one approaches from Lewes are called Blythe Cottage, Creek Cottage, Compass Cottage and Halyards—and the main street winds up past houses and cottages of various periods including a recent development of largely brick and tile-hung construction, all of which combines to present an air of unflawed picturesqueness. A frequent visitor to the landing stage by the ancient boathouse is a large, black-hulled, former fishing boat bearing the traditional Newhaven name *Economy*, whilst above and beyond it is the fish-shaped weather-vane on the church tower, the same vane of which Kipling wrote ". . . where windy Piddinghoe's beguiled dolphin veers. . . ." Certainly it can be windy in Piddinghoe when storms blow in from the Channel across the flat wastes east of Newhaven, clearly visible from the village, but Kipling rather took advantage of his artistic licence when it came to "beguiled dolphins" for the gilded weather-vane actually represents a salmon trout.

Denton, on the opposite bank of the Ouse, has become a suburb of Newhaven, its bungalows and villas climbing up the side of the Downs, whilst South Heighton and Tarring Neville immediately to the north remain farming hamlets. All three are on the B2109, which like the railway makes use of the gap in the Downs created by the Ouse to link Newhaven with Lewes. The most northerly settlement on this road is Beddingham which is a scattered agricultural parish of 280 souls with its centre at the church of St Andrew standing by a farm, a few houses and cottages and the junction of the B2109 and the A27 two miles south-east of Lewes. On the north wall of the church, the oldest part of which—the nave— is eleventh century, there is an armorial tablet bearing the name of Sir Thomas Carr who received his knighthood for performing the singularly undemanding task of conveying an address of congratulation to George III subsequent to his escaping an assassination attempt whilst at the theatre. Beddingham was united with West Firle, the adjoining parish, in 1743.

West Firle is only slightly larger than Beddingham, and more remote, being situated at the end of a lane under the Downs. It is known chiefly for Firle Place, a sixteenth-century mansion built and still owned by the Gage family, and for Firle Beacon which at 718 feet is the highest point on the Downs hereabouts. It is a dramatic spot, its history stretching into pre-recorded days, the home of Neolithic, Bronze Age and Iron Age men. A great many barrows have been discovered and excavated and relics from as late as Roman times have been found. One's fancy is easily stirred on Firle Beacon. In the *Sussex County Magazine* in 1938 a walker out on the Downs recounted how he had seen a ghostly figure coming towards him as he made his way from Firle to Beddingham one misty evening at sunset. Overcoming his initial shock and gathering his wits, he realized that the figure walked backwards as he did, forwards as he did and was identically dressed; he was, in fact, looking at a reflection of himself created by the peculiar combination of rising mist and the angle of the sun.

But it was no fancy which in the same year demolished the stone pillar on top of the beacon. During a thunderstorm a flash of lightning struck it with such force that it was split in two, one piece weighing 1 cwt. being hurled 15 feet, whilst smaller pieces were embedded in the turf all around. Fortunately no one was near enough to suffer injury, but those who witnessed the event described the flash as of such brilliance that it hid the summit. I have walked along the top of the Downs from Alfriston in the direction of Firle on a day in early spring when winter was making a dying gesture and had enveloped the heights in mist and drizzle, and it was a lonely, eerie experience, the visibility sufficient only to enable one to make out the dips of the ancient barrows and the line of fence posts disappearing into the grey, clinging dampness, the only sound the mournful hooting of fog horns in Newhaven Harbour. It was both a relief and a disappointment to descend by the road which leads down from the Beacon and come to the solid, comparatively modern cluster of cottages and houses of the village.

Further along the Downs, above the village of Wilmington, is the best-known and the most puzzling relic of the ancient inhabitants of Sussex. The controversy surrounding the origin of the Long Man of Wilmington has gone on for many years and is a fascinating one, all the more so because it is unlikely ever to be resolved. This huge figure, some 240 feet high, is a familiar landmark to travellers on the London to Eastbourne railway line and the A27. A turning off the A27 passes through Wilmington village and approaches the foot of the Long Man whence one may walk across a field to him. Since 1969 the Long Man has been marked out with white concrete blocks; prior to that white-painted bricks, 7,000 in all, had been used. These were put in place in 1874. Before the 1874 restoration he was much less clearly visible. Indeed, an old lady, Mrs Ann Downs, who died in 1928, claimed that he was really only meant to be seen at sunrise and sunset when the low angle of the sun showed up the variation in the turf.

The earliest written record of him dates only from the eighteenth century which has led to suggestions that he dates from this period, but most authorities consider him much older. However there is no agreement as to just how old he is. He resembles a somewhat smaller figure at Cerne Abbas which is known to be an ancient fertility symbol and there are links between Cerne Abbey, which was founded by Earl Godwin's great-grandfather, and Wilmington Priory, which was owned by Godwin. However the Wilmington giant also resembles figures on Roman coins and one on a seventh-century plaque found in Sweden. Then again, it has recently been suggested that he could be a Celtic surveyor holding two staves. My opinion, for what it is worth, is that the drawing of the figure—and there is some evidence to suggest that it has been modified and some features removed or lost—is too crude and basic for its resemblance to any other to be of very much significance. The revived interest in the ancient Celtic trackways lends some credence to the theory that the Wilmington giant originated during this period, and certainly there were many settlements on the Downs in Celtic times.

North of the A27, west of Firle and east of Beddingham, is

Glynde, a village set around its railway station. Like Firle it has a handsome Elizabethan manor house, built of Sussex flint and Caen stone; the estates have been owned by only four families since the days of King John. The parish church is most unusual for a Sussex village, in that it is built in the Palladian style. It was put up in 1763, replacing an earlier one. To the west of Glynde is the Caburn, an isolated hill stretching to the outskirts of Lewes and an extensive Celtic settlement occupied from 5000 B.C. until Roman times, being heavily and presumably unsuccessfully fortified against the Roman invasion. Today most visitors come to Glynde to attend the world-famous opera at Glyndebourne, a mile north of the village. The opera was founded by John Christie who came into the ownership of the house during World War I and who inaugurated the first season in 1934. From the start the greatest talents were employed, Alfred Nightingale was the manager, Fritz Busch the musical director and Carl Ebert the producer. It has never been a cheap form of entertainment and was never meant to be, involving as it did a journey in mid-afternoon by train from London, dinner in the dining room which can seat 500 people and employs over sixty waiters, and a return late at night on the Glyndebourne Opera Special. One of the additional pleasures, apart from the fine music, is to stroll through the grounds, past the buildings which contain scenery for the various productions, and amongst the extensive groves of trees.

Selmeston and Alciston, a few hundred yards north and south of the A27 respectively, are ancient hamlets with fourteenth- and thirteenth-century churches, and immediately east of them is Berwick. Its church is one of the most remarkable in the country. Many Sussex churches have fragments and a few some complete examples of medieval murals, but Berwick is unique in that its walls are covered with paintings executed in the 1940s. The Bishop of Chichester, Bishop Bell, was particularly anxious that the ancient interdependence of religion and the arts should be revived, and in 1941 he commissioned Clive Grant, Vanessa Bell and her son Quentin, all of whom had lived nearby at Firle for many years, to entirely redecorate the interior at Berwick. There was some opposition but the work went ahead and when complete met with general approval. Some of the best of it incorporates local people and scenes. In the Nativity are two local shepherds, a Pyecombe crook, the Caburn, a soldier, an airman, and a sailor from Berwick and Firle, the Bishop and the Rector.

A mile south of Berwick is Alfriston, and were there accurate statistics to prove such things it might well be that Alfriston attracts more visitors than any other village in the county. It is difficult to account for this popularity, for whilst it has a long and distinguished history and some handsome buildings in a fine setting, so do other Sussex villages. It is handily placed for mystery tours from Brighton and Eastbourne and stands on a busy road which a mile or so south of Alfriston affords a magnificent view across Seaford Bay; whatever the reason for its popularity it has not been slow to cash in on it and Alfriston possesses a quantity of tea rooms and restaurants, antique and curio shops, a zoo and pleasure gardens and a perpetual traffic problem.

Litlington lies on the opposite side of the Cuckmere, a mile to the south-east of Alfriston, and is an altogether quieter and very charming spot. Something of its atmosphere is conveyed by the following notices I once found displayed in the post office window. "The proceeds of the coffee evening in aid of family and social work came to £17." "The Women's Institute Jumble Sale raised £32·79." "The Vicar of Bishopstone wishes to thank those who helped raise £77 towards the running of the Old People's Home." "A part-time postman is required at Alfriston to work 3–5 p.m. Mondays to Fridays, wages to include a cycle cleaning allowance of 48p per week." Much of Litlington is built of flintstone, including the church of St Michael the Archangel which dates from around 1150. Although now a favourite haunt of walkers, Litlington was an out-of-the-way spot for nearly all its history and most of its inhabitants lived out their lives in peace and obscurity. An exception was Lady Fitzherbert who stayed at Clapham House and was visited there by the Prince Regent. Nothing much hap-

pened for a century or more until 1929 when London society descended on Litlington for the wedding of the daughter of Frederick
Lonsdale, now largely forgotten but at the time a West End idol
with his drawing-room comedies. The Lonsdales lived in a house
off the Litlington to Alfriston road.

Westdean is two miles south of Litlington and situated, like so
many villages in or close to the Downs, at the end of a long,
narrow lane. It is surrounded by the trees of Friston Forest, an area
of over 2,000 acres, planted by the Forestry Commission—not to
everyone's delight—in 1926. There are no shops in Westdean and
a notice at the entrance to the lane leading to it informs motorists
that there are no parking facilities. It sees plenty of traffic of a
different sort, however, for it is on the route of the South Downs
Way and on a fine Sunday dozens of walkers pass through it.
Almost all its buildings are of flintstone, including some superbly
converted stables. One of Westdean's first residents was King
Alfred and the remains of the old manor house wall south of the
church are said to be built on the site of Alfred's palace. Close
by is the Old Rectory, the earliest section of which dates from
between 1220 and 1280. It is said to be the longest continually
lived-in parsonage in the country, although very little of the
thirteenth-century fabric remains. In the church is a memorial
to Lord Waverley, in the form of a bronze head by Epstein; it was
unveiled by Harold Macmillan in 1958.

The Cuckmere valley is unusually lovely, even by Sussex stand-
ards, winding between meadows, past woods and head-high reeds,
with the Downs enclosing it, finally emerging south of Litlington
into the sea at Cuckmere Haven. Hereabouts is the only undeveloped piece of coastline between Littlehampton and Hastings, although it was a close-run thing in the 1930s. A development company applied for permission to create a pleasure beach here and
in 1936 the County Council actually granted a licence for a hotel
to be built at Exceat Bridge where the coast road crosses the
Cuckmere just over the hill from Westdean. Fortunately the
Licensing Confirmation Committee overturned this decision on the

grounds that there were no houses or residents in the neighbourhood. Three years later the peace of Exceat was again threatened
by a proposed country club and health resort consisting of brick
chalets with accommodation for 500 holiday-makers. The outbreak of war put an end to this scheme and since then the acquisition of much of the surrounding downland and clifftop area by the
National Trust has ensured Exceat's future.

Exceat was once a village; although no one knows for sure what
brought about its decline it is generally supposed that the Black
Death played a large part in it. The survivors were constantly
harassed by French raiding parties and by 1528 the inhabitants
were so few that the parish was combined with Westdean. In
1913 the site of Exceat church was discovered by E. Norman and
excavated by a group of his friends, amongst them the Rev. A. A.
Evans, vicar of the neighbouring parish of Friston and one of the
most informative and entertaining writers on Sussex. Today
Exceat consists of little more than a bridge and a farm, the steeply
inclined road on either side of the bridge giving wonderful views
over the remarkably twisting course of the Cuckmere to the
sea.

Bishopstone is three miles east of Exceat on the slope of the
Downs behind Seaford. It acquired a railway station as late as
1938 and at the time fears were expressed that this would mean
the end of the village's separate existence and its incorporation
into Seaford. Houses were certainly built close by and within a
couple of fields of the church, but that was the extent of it and
Bishopstone is not likely to lose its independence now. It is well
known, one might almost say famous, for its church, for the oldest
parts of it date back to the eighth century. The nave and the
porch belong to this period, whilst the rest is Norman; the material
for all of it is flintstone. Apart from its great historical interest
St Andrew's, Bishopstone, is a lovely church in a perfect setting
between the Downs and the sea, in full view of the main coast road
and the railway but reached only by a lane which ends beneath the
Downs. The oldest record of a windmill in Sussex, 1199, is at

Bishopstone, whilst down by the railway at Mill Creek there once stood Catt's tidal mill, the only relic of the time when the Ouse entered the sea at Seaford before it changed to its present course through Newhaven. The Catt family have a number of memorials in the church.

Over the top of the Seven Sisters on the eastern edge of Friston forest is Friston village, which is very small with its church 350 feet up by a pond where the Jevington road diverges from the A259 Brighton to Eastbourne one. The oldest parts of Friston church are Saxon; it contains several memorials to the Selwyn family who owned the Tudor Friston Place.

A few hundred yards down the hill and to the south of the main road is Eastdean, a collection of flint buildings grouped around the village green. On the opposite side of the A259, up on the Downs, is a modern development, which began in the late 1920s, of suburban type detached and semi-detached houses. The southern edge of the parish is formed by the sea and on the south-east corner is Birling Gap. Development also started here between the Wars but never amounted to very much, leaving something which is neither resort nor village. For a good many years Birling Gap was a haunt of smugglers and of those who profited from shipwrecks; the coastline hereabouts is particularly dangerous. One has only to stand on the clifftops and look down to the greenish-grey sea hurling itself at the rocks hundreds of feet below to appreciate the plight of a ship's crew wrecked here. Merely to stand close to the edge can have its dangers, as the Vicar of Eastdean discovered in 1813 when he saw a gap opening up between him and solid ground. He leapt and saved himself just in time as a section of the cliff 300 feet long and 80 feet wide vanished into the sea.

An earlier vicar, Jonathan Darby, at the beginning of the eighteenth century, took the first effective action to reduce the terrible death toll beneath the cliffs. Saddened by the number of unknown seamen buried in his churchyard, he laboriously hacked out a cave under Belle Toute cliffs above high-water mark with a tunnel and steps leading down to it, and on stormy nights he would clamber down and display a huge lantern out to sea. Many ships avoided disaster because of the Reverend Darby's steadfastness and in 1829 Belle Toute lighthouse was built directly above his cave. Storms have washed much of the cave away and the lighthouse was replaced by the more effective Beachy Head one in 1902, although its massive base survives.

Inland from Eastdean, in a dip of the Downs and within walking distance of Eastbourne, is Jevington. It has many smuggling associations and at the end of the eighteenth century the landlord of the village inn, the 'Eight Bells', one Pettit—better known as Jevington Jig—established for himself a reputation as the most notorious smuggler in the district. Many of his accomplices came to violent ends; two of them were hung outside Brighton in front of a crowd of over 10,000 for robbing a stage coach. Another was Cream-Pot Tom, who in addition to the usual commodities dealt in by the smuggling fraternity, was in the spying business, a flourishing one in Napoleonic times. Jig himself had few scruples about what he turned his hand to and nearly came to grief when he removed a load of hay from Friston one night and was arrested next morning by the law which had followed the straw trail inadvertently left by Jig. Yet such was the loyalty or more likely fear he inspired locally that the jury at Lewes refused to convict him, despite his being locked in a room without light or heat by the judge. Eventually Jig was convicted of stealing money and transported to Botany Bay.

From Jevington a narrow lane leads down to Polegate, a nineteenth-century development which grew up around the railway junction and which is now joined to Willingdon and thus to Eastbourne. East of Polegate the railway and the A27 skirt the southern edge of the Pevensey Marshes, or Levels, along a low ridge to Stonecross. There is a restored windmill here, as there is at Polegate, and until the latter part of the nineteenth century there was also one at Westham, a mile or so to the east. In 1928 a naval officer was taking bearings from the tower of St Mary's, Westham and remarked to his companion, a local man, that it was odd there was no sign of the mill used by ships as a navigation aid. He was somewhat taken aback when it was pointed out to him that they must have been confusing the Stonecross mill with the vanished Westham one for the best part of fifty years.

St Mary's, Westham (once known as West Ham), a large, flint-stone Norman church, stands at the east end of the main street which has some interesting houses of various periods, but which is overshadowed by the much better known main street of Pevensey, a few hundred yards further east.

Westham and Pevensey are separated by the massive walls of Pevensey Castle. These walls, 30 feet high in places, are largely Roman in origin and date back 1,750 years to the foundation of the Roman port of Anderida. They are made of flint, faced with sandstone and bonded with brick and ironstone. The construction and layers of the different materials can be clearly seen from the road. For miles around, to the east, the north and the south, the massive presence of the castle imposes itself upon the low-lying marshes, its only rival the gleaming dome of the Royal Greenwich Observatory at Herstmonceux, four miles to the north.

For a thousand years Pevensey was one of the principal ports of Sussex. William of Normandy landed here before the Battle of Hastings and following the Conquest its size doubled within twenty years. The town assumed considerable importance, even possessing a mint, on the site of which stands the fourteenth-century Mint House. Two factors brought about Pevensey's decline. One was the silting up of the harbour, the other the reclamation of the marshes. This latter work was completed at the end of the thirteenth century, but the danger of its being undone remained as long as the many streams and creeks which flowed across the marshes were tidal. Eventually the principal one, the Pevensey Haven, was dammed at the bridge at the eastern end of the town and without a continuous flow of water the harbour then began to silt up. Sufficient water remained in the late six-teenth century for boats of 60 tons to enter and Pevensey re-

mained a corporate member of the Cinque Ports, but it was by
then little more than a village.

In its later years as a port Pevensey played its part in the iron
trade, particularly during the winter when roads became impass-
able and the iron was sent by barge along the marsh ditches to
warehouses at Pevensey Bridge, whence it was exported to the
Continent and beyond. But the erection of further dams and
sluices, coupled with the natural eastward drift of the English
Channel, which built up a bank of shingle along the shores of
Pevensey Bay, finally ended Pevensey's days as a port. The castle
fell into ruins and a good deal of its masonry was put to other
uses, although the largest part remains intact and it was briefly
brought back into use as a strongpoint during World War II. The
sea is now more than a mile from the village and the castle,
although the marshes are still liable to flood, and at the time of
the ferocious storms of February 1974 it was possible to look from
the landing window of my father's house in Hailsham across a
practically continuous sheet of water stretching to the sea.

Pevensey Bay is a twentieth-century development of beach huts,
bungalows, a hotel, shops and two churches, strung out along the
edge of the shingle beach towards Eastbourne and Bexhill. It is
not very beautiful—indeed the official guide to the Rural District
of Hailsham, predecessor of the Wealden Council which adminis-
ters the area, describes it as a "hideous fringe". This is rather
hard for the bungalows are generally well cared for, often with
flourishing gardens magically conjured out of the pebbles, and in
a quiet sort of way Pevensey Bay with the sea before it and the
lonely, untouched marshes behind is not without its attractions.

The chief inhabitants of the marshes are sheep, cattle and
"lookers", the latter followers of an ancient occupation of looking
after the sheep of the often absentee landlords. Some dismiss the
marshes as dull, missing their subtle changes of mood; three of
England's greatest artists were certainly captivated by them,
Samuel Palmer, Constable and Turner all painting them. Wartling

is the only village actually on the marshes but Hooe lies on their eastern fringes whilst Magham Down, Herstmonceux, Windmill Hill, Boreham Street and Ninfield all overlook them from the ridge to the north along which the A271 Lewes to Hastings road runs.

Many of their inhabitants indulged in smuggling in former days, dealing not only in wines and spirits but also in wool. Until Tudor times when it became more profitable to turn the land over to sheep pasture the marshes had been fairly densely populated by tenant farmers. They lived in what had of necessity to be a close-knit community, each depending upon his neighbour to ensure that the dykes and streams which passed through his land were kept clear in order that the whole of the marshes might be properly drained. Salt-panning had by then ceased—Domesday records that there were thirteen pans in the parish of Hailsham and four each in the neighbouring ones of Bowley and Hooe—but mixed farming and fishing ensured a reasonable degree of prosperity.

The period from the end of the Black Death until Tudor times was a prosperous one for labourers who, following the decimation of the population after the plague, found their services in great demand. Wages rose, although this did not prevent many men from the marshes joining Jack Cade's Revolt in 1452, amongst them the bailiff and burgesses of Pevensey, but, by the Dissolution, the economic climate had changed and many of the tenant farmers found themselves without homes or land. In the sixteenth century a law was passed forbidding the export of wool, but it was one which was difficult to enforce in a district like the marshes with so easy an access to the sea, and the landowners made their fortunes. In 1531 upwards of 150,000 packs of wool were smuggled out of England, a good proportion of them passing over the Pevensey Marshes. No doubt the actual transporting was carried out by the tenants who had lost their livelihoods, for it was a period when many able-bodied men could find no legal employment. The penalty was usually gibbeting, the body being left on the shore for the seabirds, but with starvation or emigration the alternative, there was no shortage of those willing to run the risk and the trade continued to Napoleonic times.

The population has never really recovered from the effects of the Black Death and the pasturation of the marshes, and although Hailsham has expanded enormously of late, the marsh area remains largely uninhabited and the villages on its perimeter small. It is possible to wander for half the day along marsh roads, at times being less than a mile from the crowded beaches of Pevensey and Normans Bay, and yet encounter no more than a dozen vehicles and pass less than half that number of dwellings. Wartling, although once possessed of an RAF camp, remains small and off the beaten track, and even Herstmonceux, although visually significant and a place of great astronomical importance, is not very large. In 1948 the Royal Greenwich Observatory moved from smoky London to the clear skies of Sussex, took over Herstmonceux Castle and erected a number of buildings and structures in the grounds, including six steel and copper domes and a huge telescope, which latter dominates the marshes. The De Monceux family came over from Normandy with the Conqueror, but the castle was not begun until 1441, by which time the manor had passed to Roger Fiennes, who fought at Agincourt. In the eighteenth century the castle was allowed to decay but was restored between 1911 and 1935. It is similar in design to Bodiam and has a moat, but perhaps because it is complete and still occupied it lacks Bodiam's decayed but evocative grandeur. Herstmonceux possesses a handsome twelfth-century church, immediately west of the castle and some distance south of the village with a fine view from it across the marshes to Hailsham and to the Downs behind Beachy Head. Magham Down is no more than a hamlet which might well one day be swallowed up by Hailsham, whilst Windmill Hill and Boreham Street are small, main-road villages each with a mixture of old and modern cottages and houses and with extensive views southwards across the marshes to the sea and northwards over the rolling Weald.

Trug-making is an industry unique to the Herstmonceux dis-

trict. A trug is a shallow wooden basket chiefly used by gardeners; it is said to be traditional although its recorded history goes
back no further than the middle of the last century. In 1851
Thomas Smith, a trug-maker of Herstmonceux, walked to Hyde
Park to exhibit a trug in the Great Exhibition. This piece of enter-
prise was rewarded by an order from Queen Victoria and since
then trug-making has been an established business in and around
the village.

·Hooe is a straggling, largely twentieth-century village, although
it has an isolated fifteenth-century church standing on the edge
of the marshes. It is not the sort of place which attracts many
visitors, but it is not without interest. I once, whilst looking
around an old barn, came across an immaculate bullnose Morris
Cowley, all but fifty years old, standing in a corner amongst the
straw, and one also occasionally encounters horse-drawn vehicles
in the district; the pleasant sounds of jingling harnesses and rumbling cart-wheels can still be heard on marsh roads.

Ninfield stands at the junction of the Battle, Bexhill, Pevensey
and Hailsham roads. Red brick predominates here; there is little
stonework in any of the marsh villages. The parish church,
approached through an archway of trees, dates from the thirteenth
century but has been rebuilt and repaired many times since then.
Amongst the memorials is one to a Red Cross nurse of the First
World War, Barbara Esmee St John, who died in France in 1916
and was buried at the soldiers' cemetery at Wimereux. Above the
clock, made at the Midland Steam Clock Works in Derby in 1898,
is a seventeenth-century minstrel's gallery, although how one
reaches it is a mystery for there is no visible means of access.
Beside the church is the National School, beyond this the Methodist church with a carved wooden figure which I take to be John
Wesley, and at the end of the road the old iron stocks on the
Green.

This distant view of Catsfield, two miles to the east on the
Battle road, is remarkable in that it is dominated not by the
parish church as are so many villages, but by the tall spire

Looking along the Pevensey Haven towards the ramparts of the castle and the church

The Saxon church at Bishopstone

The Herstmonceux telescope, seen from Wartling

A view of Fairlight from the church tower

The wide main street at Winchelsea

The restored interior of East Guldeford Church

Northiam, roses and weather-boarding

A meeting of the cycling club at Frant

Sedlescombe, home of the
Pestalozzi Children's Village

The twelfth-century church at
Guestling

Victorian non-conformism at Robertsbridge

Ticehurst on a foggy December morning

The main street at Mayfield

Rotherfield

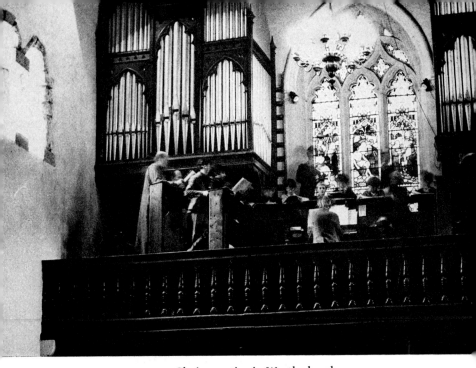

Choir practice in Worth church

Hartfield during a March snowstorm

of the Methodist one. It is a very Gothic building, put up in 1912. The parish church of St Lawrence goes back to 1190. It lies to the south of the village centre, hidden amongst a bank of trees, and as in a number of country churches Evensong begins earlier in winter than in summer. Thomas Brassy, the greatest of the pioneer railway contractors, is buried in the churchyard. He built railways in many parts of Britain and further afield, but, rather curiously, none in his home county. The nearest station to Catsfield is Crowhurst, on the Hastings line, a small village notable for two things: its Home of Healing, founded by the Rev Howard Cobb in 1928 after his recovery from an apparently incurable disease; and its ancient yew trees. These latter are said to be amongst the most ancient in existence. It is impossible to date them precisely, but the circumference of the largest tree at Crowhurst, at a height of 5 feet from the ground, is 28 feet, and thus according to Kew Gardens it is somewhere between 1,000 and 3,000 years old.

South of Crowhurst is the coast with Bexhill merging into St Leonards and St Leonards into Hastings. East of Hastings the cliffs have been made a national park, and thus Fairlight, which stands at the end of them, has retained its independence, although from Fairlight onwards, through Cliff End, Pett Level, Winchelsea Beach, past the mouth of the Rother and as far as Camber Sands, there is a succession of unplanned caravan sites, chalets, the odd café and shop, and one or two remaining converted railway carriages. The parish church of Fairlight with its 82-foot high tower is a tremendous landmark set on top of the cliffs, which hereabouts rise 536 feet out of the sea. It is an important navigation point, which is open to the public at certain times and from which it is possible to see right across the Channel to the French coast and Boulogne, whilst landwards one may look beyond Rye to the Walland and Romney marshes and over the Weald past Robertsbridge and Bodiam to Tunbridge Wells. Fairlight Lodge, built on top of the cliffs in front of the church, is said to have belonged originally to a French refugee count who was a smuggler; at night,

K

when the coast was clear, he shone a lantern from one of the lodge windows. One of the most popular paintings of the last century, 'The Strayed Sheep' by Holman Hunt, is set on the clifftop at Fairlight, whilst another household name of the period, Richard D'Oyly Carte, is buried in the churchyard.

The present Fairlight church was built in 1845, replacing a twelfth-century one which was in danger of collapse and which in any case had grown too small for the needs of the parish. Fairlight has continued to expand and a few years ago a second, temporary church was erected down the hill below the old one. The parish church stands in Coastguard Lane, opposite the old school. The school-house belongs to the verger, the school buildings being empty following the school's amalgamation with Guestling and Pett in 1955, since which time the children all go to Guestling Green.

In a recess in the cliffs below Fairlight church is the Lovers' Seat, a name said by some to be a reminder of a romantic but tragic story. The truth is that it was romantic certainly but not tragic. The lieutenant of a revenue cutter and a local heiress fell in love. Her parents, not foreseeing any chance of his making much of a mark in the world, forbade the match, but the lovers contrived to meet beneath the cliffs. They eloped, married in London, received the parents' forgiveness, and lived happily ever after.

Guestling is a large village, strung out along and to the west of the A259 Hastings to Folkestone road. At the south-eastern extremity, deep in the countryside, is the beautiful little parish church of St Laurence which was founded by John de Gestling in the twelfth century. The west end of Guestling is within sight of and almost connected to the Hastings suburb of Ore. Icklesham, two miles east of Guestling along the A259, is a good deal smaller, despite having doubled its population in the last ten years. Many of its new inhabitants are retired people from London, but others, as do a good few from Guestling, Westfield, Winchelsea and Rye, work in either Hastings or Ashford. The Hastings to Ashford railway line was on the point of imminent closure for many years, but a vigorous campaign by the local people outwitted British Rail and its survival seems assured.

There is documentary reference to Icklesham as far back as A.D. 772; the village takes its name from Icel, a Saxon chief. In ancient times it was a good deal more important than it is now and the hill on which Winchelsea now stands was within its parish, as was Rye Harbour. The interior of the parish church of All Saints is particularly fine; when I last saw it, it looked unusually attractive for it was the Saturday before Harvest Festival and the vicar and the parishioners were filling the windows, ledges, steps and floor with an abundance of local produce, which included hops. Icklesham, like many Sussex village churches, possesses decorated hassocks. The Icklesham ones are of four designs, a red rose, a fish, a sheep and a ship, each one embroidered by a lady of the parish.

The parish church of Pett, like that at Fairlight, is a prominent mark from both land and sea. It, too, is a Victorian replacement of a much older one. Pett village is a mixture of old and new, but Pett Level, behind the sea wall of Rye Bay, is an entirely twentieth-century development, continuing eastwards until it becomes Winchelsea Beach. The sea wall is high enough to force motorists to stop and climb the wall if they want a view of the sea, but it is worth the effort for one may look right across the bay to the nuclear power station at Dungeness, which possesses its own sort of beauty; or one may turn inland towards the infinitely older sight of sheep grazing on the marshes in front of the wooded hill on which Winchelsea stands, with the almost overpoweringly picturesque town of Rye beyond.

Winchelsea, like Pevensey, is a once busy port from which the sea has departed leaving a village where formerly there was a town, a village full of reminders of great days gone for ever. It has an air of timelessness as though the gods had decided that it had reached perfection and should be preserved in such a state, nothing within it changing regardless of growth and decay in the world outside. The nearest navigable water is more than a mile away and it is almost impossible to reconcile Winchelsea's present moribund—if exquisite—state with that of its former one of a great port. William I landed here on his return to England a year after the Conquest, but even then its decline had begun, for its harbour was slowly silting up, and when a succession of gales brought further destruction Edward I decided to rebuild the town three miles to the north-west on a piece of high ground almost surrounded by water. The new Winchelsea, construction of which began in July 1288, was admitted, along with Rye, to full membership of the Cinque Ports Federation. It was laid out in the French manner in a series of squares covering 39 acres, but it was never completed on account of French raids and the alteration in the course of the Rother, and although the grid of streets remains, much of the 39 acres is grassland and the buildings which still stand are almost all residential.

Every house and cottage in Winchelsea is in a superb state of preservation, but none can compare with the partially ruined but magnificent church of St Thomas. Its interior is particularly fine and some would claim that its chief glory is the series of stained-glass windows, possibly the best in Sussex; they are the exception which proves the rule that everything of beauty in Winchelsea is ancient. They were designed by Douglas Strachan and given by Lord Blanesburgh in the early 1930s in memory of his brothers and nephews and as a memorial, in the words of the inscription, "To the men of the Cinque Ports and the ancient towns of Rye and Winchelsea, who whether on sea or land or in the air, gave their lives in the War, 1914–1918, and in thanksgiving for those who returned safe to their homes."

# 9

## Furthest East

TUCKED away in the furthest corner of East Sussex is Camber, which, like its counterpart, Bracklesham, in the furthest west, is a twentieth-century development of caravans and bungalows, with a fine sandy beach. Even the church is modern, scarcely twenty years old, although it looks rather more venerable. There is an ancient part of Camber—the Castle—but as this is on the opposite bank of the Rother and involves a detour into Rye, one tends not to associate it with the modern Camber. Camber Castle was occupied for barely 100 years. It was one of a series erected by Henry VIII to protect the south coast against a possible French invasion, and when both this threat, and the sea, had receded, it was given up in 1642. Its exterior walls survive, largely intact, and its curiously geometric shape of a circular keep surrounded by four almost completely circular towers and a circular gatehouse may be clearly noted.

East of Camber Castle, west of Camber Sands, and north of them both is East Guldeford. Its parish church of St Mary is often described as lonely, and as much as it stands by itself in a field and the flat expanses of Romney Marsh extend to its south and east, I suppose it is. Yet both Rye and Playden are little more than a mile distant to the west and north respectively and clearly visible on the high ground above the marsh, whilst the very busy A259 coastal road and the Hastings to Ashford railway line are a good deal nearer. Perhaps St Mary's loneliness is more apparent in winter than in summer. Be that as it may, East Guldeford church is exquisite. There can hardly be a simpler one in all Sussex. It is built of brick, which is unusual for there are only two other brick churches of similar antiquity—Egdean and Twineham—in the county, and because it is sixteenth century, the bricks are only 9 inches by 2 inches, smaller than those now standard, and are laid in the old English style of alternate courses of stretchers and headers. In its plainness St Mary's has something of the feeling of a large barn; the interior is all one with no division between the chancel and nave. In 1929 when the Rev. A. A. Evans visited East Guldeford he wrote in the *Sussex County Magazine* that the church was in need of repair; it has taken a long time but the work of restoration is now almost complete and has been most beautifully done. Particularly noticeable is the condition of the wood and brick floor, the vestry partition and the eighteenth-century pine box pews. The completion of this and other work coincided with Architectural Heritage Year and earned for the church an award from the Civic Trust.

Except when a service is on, St Mary's is locked, but the massive key is kept in a nearby house and is readily available to visitors. The reader may have noticed the similarity between the name of the village and that of Guildford, in Surrey, and although villagers have been quoted as saying that there is no connection this is not, strictly speaking true. In fact the land was bought in 1480 by Sir Richard Guldeford, a member of an ancient family which took its name from Guildford, Surrey, and the first recorded instance of the name in Sussex is of Newguldford. Sir Richard bought what at high tide was an expanse of sea. He drained the land, put up a sea wall and built cottages for the marshmen. He died in Jerusalem whilst on a pilgrimage to the Holy Land. He had set out from Rye but his family home was at Hemsted in Kent; the title became extinct in 1740. There were never many parishioners living on the Guldeford estates in Sussex, the number in 1676 being thirty-five. Today it is around a hundred. In 1746 East Guldeford was incorporated into the parish of Playden; even so it was hardly possible to find all the money locally to pay for the extensive restorations which had for so long been necessary, and the present excellent state of the church is largely due to the Sussex Historic Churches Trust and the Historic Churches Preservation Trust which together in 1972 decided to finance the work.

Playden, the parent parish of East Guldeford, is a much larger village, and is almost joined on to Rye, which lies due south of it. It is a prosperous-looking place, in a fine setting with extensive views over Rye and the Romney Marshes. The parish church of St Michael is very largely twelfth century with a more modern, handsome spire, which is a landmark for many miles to the south and east. Playden's proximity to Rye and the sea has added some cosmopolitan touches, including a good deal of either French or French-influenced decoration in the church. In the north aisle there is the ledger gravestone of Cornelius Zoetmanns, a Flemish brewer. Until the late fourteenth century the English drank ale, but from that time beer began to be imported from the Netherlands, first of all through Winchester and Rye. Breweries were established and no doubt Zoetmanns came over for this reason. A much later resident from abroad was Henry James, who wrote *The Spoils of Poynton* in Playden. One of the last tolls in Sussex was imposed on traffic plying along a road near the Star Inn; they were still being charged in 1936, wagons having to pay one shilling, carts sixpence.

Iden is two miles due north of Playden on the B2082 which leads to the beautiful Kent town of Tenterden. This latter is the focal point for the surrounding Kent and Sussex villages. Iden extends for some distance along either side of the main road, and the parish church of All Saints is part Norman, part Perpendicular.

The London road leaves Rye by way of Playden, branches to the left at the north of the village, leaving the Tenterden road to continue on through Iden and across the border, and arrives at Peasmarsh. Its church is quite isolated from the village, up a lane to the south-west, the principal part of Peasmarsh being strung out along the main road. It goes back at least a thousand years, although a good deal of it now consists of fairly modern bungalows. Amongst them, right in the village centre, is a group of far older single-storey weather-boarded cottages, and here and there are other old houses.

It is recorded that Count Robert of Eu gave the church to his grandson Henry, soon after the Conquest, and the nave, chancel arch and part of the chancel date from around 1070. The interior of the church has a rather worn, slightly impoverished look, although this is probably more noticeable than it might be in that the windows let in a good deal more light than do those of many Sussex village churches. The chancel arch is built of distinctive iron sandstone and about head high on each is carved the figure of an unidentifiable animal. Outside in the churchyard is the Liddell grave. The family lived at Peasmarsh Place, and the pulpit, altar rails, east window and the church lighting were given by them. However, they are chiefly celebrated on account of Alice Liddell, for whom Lewis Carroll first related *Alice's Adventures in Wonderland*.

South of Peasmarsh is Rye Foreign, a hamlet which was once part of the parish of Rye. The A268 London road continues north-westwards towards the Kent border, but if we turn left at Four Oaks we can make a detour which will take us through Beckley and Northiam, and bring us back to the main road just before it crosses the Kent and East Sussex railway and the Rother which marks the border.

Beckley extends for quite a distance along the ridge upon which the road is built, although it is not very large, its houses and cottages being well spread out. It ends at the church which stands in a commanding position at the top of a hill, with a view across the valley to Northiam, not much more than a mile distant. A wooded lane dips steeply down on one side of the church whilst the Northiam road swings round to the south-west. Opposite, standing amongst trees, in the early eighteenth-century Church House, and a little further along is a recently erected, partly weather-boarded house on the opposite side of the road from the

Old Forge tea-house. It is a delightfully peaceful spot, rarely disturbed by any excess of traffic.

Beckley is mentioned in Alfred the Great's will of the late ninth century. The oldest surviving building is the herring-bone stone church tower, the lowest part of which was completed in 1150. The rest of the church, All Saints, is largely thirteenth century, with a fine east window notable for its reticulated tracery, erected around 1320. The church chest is from 1480, or possibly earlier, and, as can clearly be seen, was dug out of a tree trunk. It is bound round with Sussex iron and originally served as the church safe. The Lady Chapel is also known as the Knelle Chapel, being at one time the burial place of the family of that name who were the ancient lords of the manor. Great Knelle, their eighteenth-century home, is to the north of the village, whilst the much older fifteenth-century Knelle Dower House is a short distance to the west of the church. There is an attractive lych gate at the east end of the churchyard with the carved figures of a knight in armour on one side, an angel with a sword on the other, and Christ above. It was erected by Charles and Mary Bates in memory of their two sons, and "all our fighting men" who died in World War I. By the gate are the graves of two rectors of Beckley, the Rev. Hugh Wilson, who died in 1961, and his successor, the Rev. Edward Sporne, who died two years later.

Northiam, which may be clearly seen from Beckley, is one of the largest and most handsome of Sussex villages. Its long main street contains a rich variety of houses of all periods. There is a lot of weather-boarding, but also a good deal of timber-framed brick and plaster, tile-hung, brick, white-painted Victorian plaster over brick, and modern brick. There is what is claimed to be the "largest wooden house in England", although whether this is the handsome three-storied weather-boarded estate agent's in front of the church, or the equally large timber-framed house opposite, is difficult to determine. The church of St Mary is set back a little from the main road, on a rise and partly hidden by buildings. On the Green to one side of these buildings is a famous oak tree. It is reputed to be

1,000 years old and is corseted round with a stout iron chain; however this is not its chief claim to fame. On 11 August 1573 Queen Elizabeth I stayed in Northiam and she sat under the tree and there changed her shoes. Northiam seemingly pleased her and as a memento, she left the shoes, of green damask silk, behind her. They are still kept in the village and are displayed on special occasions. A little way along the road, on the opposite side, the gates of the playing field commemorate the visit in May 1944 of four prime ministers, Higgins of Southern Rhodesia, Mackenzie King of Canada, Smuts of South Africa and Winston Churchill. At the back of one of the houses opposite the church I found a big, high-standing four-wheel wagon. Its owner told me it was known as a Sussex wagon, although a mile or so down the road on the other side of the Rother it would be known as a Kent wagon! It had been brought up from a farm by the railway and was around fifty years old. It was in excellent condition although it had not been used for some twenty years and the nearest horses at present at work on a farm were over at Hurst Green, six miles away. Working horses may have gone from Northiam, although there are plenty around for riding, but dogs and other pets are especially welcome, if that is quite the word, in the Blue Cross St Francis Field of Rest behind the Crown and Thistle. Another of Northiam's pubs, the Six Bells, is said to be one of the oldest in England, although it has been much modernized. Close to the Crown and Thistle the National Westminster Bank somewhat unusually had a display of paintings by small children in its window on one of my recent visits to the village. Equally unusual was the fact that not one shop was open, the best Northiam could offer being a lock-up garage selling papers. Admittedly it was a Sunday, but it was also summertime and there are very few villages, certainly of the size of Northiam, which do not consider it worthwhile opening at least one general shop and a tea-house when there are visitors about. As if this were not enough I found the church locked up less than half an hour after Matins was over. Less curious were the locked doors of a small non-conformist chapel at the

north end of the village, for I was informed by a resident standing at his gate a couple of doors down the street that the size of
the congregation had dwindled to the point where it could no
longer afford to keep the chapel open. He added that it was typical
of what was happening all over the county and I agreed with him
out of politeness, but it is not really so. The parish church is still
very much the centre of life in the great majority of Sussex villages,
even if the peripheral activities attached to it, such as the Women's
Institute, Mother's Union, Scouts, Guides, etc. sometimes attract
more regular adherents than the actual services.

St Mary's, Northiam is a fine church, mostly built of ironstone.
A large part of the nave and the chancel is fourteenth century,
whilst the lower part of the tower is probably a century older. The
tall spire, unusual in that it is of stone, dates from the first years
of the sixteenth century, whilst a large part of the east end of the
church was rebuilt and extended in the year of Queen Victoria's
accession to the throne. Nine years later the ornate mausoleum of
the Frewen family was erected by Sydney Smirke. The Frewens
were the lords of the manor and one of their homes was Church
House, a lovely mansion built by John Frewen, who was rector from
1598 to 1628. It has a later, early eighteenth-century brick façade
and stands immediately to the north of the church.

The northern end of Northiam is fairly modern with a number of
detached houses, many built in the 1920s and 1930s. They possess
no great architectural merit, although they are pleasant enough
in their way. No doubt when they were new and had not yet settled
into the landscape they did little for the character of the village.
Certainly the Rev. A. A. Evans, usually a most sensitive and sympathetic writer, declared in the *Sussex County Magazine* in 1937
that the widening of the road through Northiam and the putting
of too good a surface on it had attracted cheap builders. Perhaps
he had had trouble composing his sermon that morning for he gave
poor Northiam something of a roasting, remarking scathingly that
its title "Queen of Sussex villages" was "fatuous". He did concede,
however, that parts of it were "pleasing and gracious". They are

indeed and few villages possess such a high proportion of handsome buildings and glorious gardens.

North of Northiam the main road joins the A268 Rye to London road, and then crosses the Rother and enters the Kent village of Newenden. Immediately before the border it passes over a level crossing; the railway is the Kent and East Sussex, the second of the steam preservation projects in the county to come to fruition. The Bluebell experienced a fairly painless birth, but the Kent and East Sussex, or the Rother Valley as it is also known, had to fight for its life for years. It had never really known prosperity, except for brief periods at hop-picking time, when thousands of Londoners made the journey to the hop fields of the Kent and Sussex border country around Northiam, and had remained in private owner-ship until nationalized in 1948. It had been built, like the Selsey Tramway, by Col. Stephens, and originally ran from Robertsbridge to Headcorn, through lovely but not very densely populated coun-try; the only town it served was Tenterden. In order to keep costs down there were few bridges and a great many level crossings. It was these latter which proved such a stumbling block to its re-opening, for it was claimed that great delays would be caused to motorists held up by trains crossing the roads. There were some who felt that the motorists were so adept at delaying themselves that there was little the occasional train could do to add to the congestion; in the event the years of work carried out by volun-teers, including a number of schoolchildren, came to fruition in 1974 when the line reopened. Ironically no trains were running on British Rail on the day of the reopening owing to an industrial dispute and so the Kent and East Sussex attracted nationwide publicity. At present only a short section is in operation, but much work has been done along the line and at the stations at Northiam and Bodiam and it is hoped to run services to them soon.

Bodiam is known far and wide for its magnificent castle. The village is small, immediately to the west of the castle, and the church is up a hill to the north. The original manor house at Bodiam was fortified in 1385, following the burning of Rye in

1377, and Winchelsea three years later: It stood guarding the Rother, which provided virtually the only means of communication between that part of the country and the coast through the undulating, thickly wooded landscape; indeed as late as the 1930s coal and timber barges sailed to Bodiam from Rye. Bodiam Castle probably fell into disuse at the time of the Civil War; its preservation—as a very impressive ruin—is usually credited to Lord Curzon, who owned it from 1918 to his death in 1926, but although he certainly did carry out preservation work and ensured its future by bequeathing it to the National Trust, this hardly does justice to his predecessor. He was the first Baron Ashcombe, a member of the great architectural and civil engineering Cubitt family. His father, Thomas Cubitt, built the Manor House as a rectory for his daughter and son-in-law, the Rev. C. Palmer, and Lord Ashcombe bought the castle in 1864. He started the restoration work and had done a good deal by the time the Castle and the Manor House passed into the ownership of Lord Curzon.

One approaches Bodiam Castle through a gateway down by the river and arrives at it by climbing up a grassy slope. The immediate impression the Castle presents is of a great mass of windows and doorways, towering up above the moat, which is kept beautifully clean and teams with fish. To enter the castle one has to walk round two sides of it to the north entrance which is reached by a causeway, divided into two by an islet. The height of the 6 feet 6 inches thick walls is 41 feet, whilst the circular towers at each corner exceed 60 feet. Not much of the original house, upon which the fortifications were built, survives, but there is enough to show us what it must have been like. There were living rooms, a buttery, kitchen and pantry, the doorways to each of which remain, a large hall, bedrooms in the north-east tower, a sacristy and a chapel, the latter possessing the largest window in the castle. One may still climb to the top of a tower and look out over the valley of the Rother to Northiam to the south, across the meadows to the east and north, and to the red-brick and tile-hung houses of the village to the west. From the outside Bodiam

Castle looks almost complete and the ruined state of its interior serves only to heighten its grandeur.

The parish church of St Giles, almost hidden amongst trees, possesses that rare treasure, a handsome nineteenth-century stained glass window, in glowing reds, blues and greens, dedicated to one of the Cubitt family. The roof, rather unusually, steepens halfway up, and equally rare are the upholstered seats of the pews. St Giles is a fourteenth-century church, which was restored in the nineteenth century. This restoration is thought in some circles to have been the ruin of it; if it was it must have been quite exceptional in its original state for St Giles is still in its simple, unpretentious way a lovely little church.

If we retrace our steps back to Rye and then leave it by way of the level crossing by the station we find ourselves on a road which runs on a ridge parallel to that which carries the Northiam one and which will bring us to Udimore. The guidebook to the church is the most distinctive I have come across in all Sussex. The text, instead of being set in type, is reproduced in manuscript lettering, and is liberally illustrated with some very nice line drawings, reproductions and photographs. The guide relates the legend concerning the building of the church, how it was begun down on marshy land, how the foundations disappeared each night so that the parishioners determined to stay up to see what was going on, "And behold the air was filled with the rushing and glistening wings of angels who took the stones of the church and carried them over the water. As they did so the night winds bore back the chant to the onlookers: Over the mere! Over the mere!" It is suggested that this was how the original name of the village, Uddy-mere, originated, although it is admitted that there is at least one other church which claims the legend, and other explanations for the name.

St Mary's is a Norman church, heavily rebuilt in the thirteenth century and altered again in the nineteenth. The manor belonged to the Etchingham family—the village of Etchingham is ten miles to the west—and in Norman and later times they lived at Court

Lodge, which adjoined the church. I met an old man tending his parents' grave in the churchyard who told me he had known the old house and how when it was demolished he had watched the massive timbers and the pegs which held them being removed. He was a mine of information, as old inhabitants of villages always are, although equally one has to be careful to distinguish fact from legend and hearsay. A large brick cow shed beside the church he described, like the derelict manor house, as being "very old"; in fact it bore the date 1878. He told me that at the beginning of winter the calves were driven into the shed and into deep pits filled with straw. The fall did them no harm but they were unable to get out until the next spring, by which time they had grown sufficiently to climb out. It sounded a cruelly simple method of fattening cattle, but it is foolish for non-farming people to criticize treatment of animals if they do not have the country person's understanding of them. At any rate although the shed was still used by cattle, the pits had all been boarded over. Growing close by the shed was an oak tree, its trunk and lower branches practically engulfed by an elderberry bush, but once it had provided a fine roasting place for turkeys. The gallows used to stand on the opposite side of the church from the farm, now there is a field of black currants, with the village green beyond.

It is salutary to be reminded of the state of St Mary's Church immediately before its restoration in Victorian times, a restoration much criticized, like so many others in Sussex. "There had been no Communion Service for three years—the walls were damp, the timbers rotten, the tower unsafe, the floor uneven and mean, the ceiling full of holes, the bells cracked, the windows broken and the font a sixpenny pudding basin." Inevitably some of the restoration work was clumsy and insensitive, but much of this has been put right over the succeeding eighty years, and, much more important, it prevented the complete physical and spiritual collapse of the parish which might otherwise have occurred.

The road continues from Udimore to Broad Oak, a largely modern development of bungalows and houses set around a crossroads, and to Brede, to which parish Broad Oak belongs. Brede has its place in history for the movement began there in 1830 which led to the reform of the Poor Law and the slow improvement of the lot of the farm labourer, which at that time was probably worse than at any period since the Conquest. More than half the population of the parish was on relief and the master of the workhouse, Thomas Abell, was a particularly unpleasant character. One of the tasks he set the inmates—men and women—was to harness them to a heavy cart, send it down to the wharf beside the River Brede, load it up with stones from the barges tied up there, and then have it hauled up the hill to the village. This treatment, coupled with the general resentment felt throughout the county at high rents and taxes and the introduction of machinery on the land, stretched the forbearance of the people of Brede too far. On 4th April 1830, 500 of them, with the support of the local farmers, invited Abell to sit in his own cart, which was then pulled to Robertsbridge where he was dumped by the roadside and left. It says much for the Brede people that Abell escaped so lightly. This signalled the beginning of a widespread revolt throughout Sussex and beyond, with much rick burning and smashing of machinery.

One of the causes of unemployment in Brede was, first, the decline of the iron industry, and then after the Napoleonic War, the end of the gunpowder mills. Guns were cast in Brede as late as 1760 and taken down by barge to Winchelsea Gun Wharf. When the furnace closed in 1766 it was converted into a powder mill and this continued in operation until 1825. There is practically nothing to see now for the buildings were demolished and the ponds drained for hop fields, although some of the bay remains. As may be imagined, manufacturing gunpowder was a hazardous business. In the early years of the mill there was an accident in which one of the workers was "blown apart", and a little later in July 1787 another explosion killed one man and severely injured another. In Westfield, two miles away, the villagers described the impact as being "like the shock of an earthquake". Westfield is a big village, much of it belonging to the twentieth century, a result of its proximity to Hastings and its position on the A28 Hastings to Canterbury and Margate road, but it has a long history. The Romans worked iron here, whilst the parish church of St John the Baptist retains a good deal of Norman work.

Sedlescombe, north-west of Westfield on the A229 Hastings to Maidstone and Chatham road, is the most picturesque village in the district. It lies in a valley, its houses and cottages built on either side of the long, narrow green which extends up a steep hill. Much of Sedlescombe dates from the sixteenth and seventeenth centuries when the iron industry made it prosperous. The oldest part of the church, built on a bank above the road at the northern end of the village, is fourteenth century, with many additions since then. Oaklands, a mansion around which the Pestalozzi International Village was built in the 1950s and 1960s, was designed by Decimus Burton, the son of the founder of Bexhill which is some seven miles distant. Titus Oates went to school at Sedlescombe in the 1660s; in 1876 a hoard of silver coins, all minted during the reign of Edward the Confessor, was dug up near the school. They are thought to have belonged to King Harold and been buried after the Battle of Hastings, Battle being but three miles away.

Few Sussex villages are in greater need of a bypass than Robertsbridge, for the A21 runs right through its middle. At weekends private cars and coaches are almost nose to tail, whilst during the week there is a constant flow of heavy lorries, many of them bound for or coming away from the British Gypsum works three miles distant at Mountfield. Although it does not seem to have happened, one would hardly be surprised if the inhabitants living on the east side of the main street regarded those on the west as virtual foreigners and vice versa. Probably the most dangerous crossing place is opposite Salehurst Primary School at the north end of the village where Robertsbridge and Salehurst meet on a blind corner and where some genius has built a pavement on the inside of the curve but not on the outside, thereby forcing pedestrians to take their lives in their hands each time they negotiate it.

L

Such a preamble might lead the reader to conclude that Roberts-bridge is best avoided; this certainly is not so for in many ways it is in the first rank of Sussex villages. Traffic apart, the main street is a delight, a well-matched mixture of red-tiled, boarded and timber-framed houses set on a winding hill. The National Westminster Bank is housed in a gem of a white-painted, boarded cottage facing the road which leads down to the station a quarter of a mile distant, whilst a few doors away on either side, as though to ensure the villagers retain a strict sense of values, are non-conformist places of worship. The Bethel Strict Baptist Chapel of 1842 is indeed a strict-looking affair, but the United Reformed Church up the road was put up all but forty years later and is thus a gothicized Italianate extravaganza. It might be argued that this latter strikes a somewhat jarring note, but it might equally be claimed that it adds a welcome touch of Mediterranean bravura not usually found amongst the discreet delights of a Sussex village.

Members of the established church have a good deal further to go, for the parish church of Robertsbridge is actually in Sale-hurst, the adjoining village to the north-east. On the north side of the Salehurst Road is a neat post-war development, partly private, partly council, including Coronation Cottages, whilst to the south across the meadows flanking the Rother are hop fields and oast houses. There is hardly enough of Salehurst to warrant the title village; apart from the church there is a post office, a pub called the Old Eight Bells (the new Eight Bells is back on the A21 prac-tically in Robertsbridge) and a few houses. A nearby farm incor-porates the remains of Robertsbridge Abbey, a Cistercian establish-ment founded in 1176 by Robert de St Martin; he it was who gave his name to the village.

The church of St Mary the Virgin is at least visible through the trees from Robertsbridge even if some distance from it. It has a rather heavy-looking tower dating from around 1250 and heightened some 150 years later and a plain but impressive in-terior with an unusually long nave. In the entrance under the tower is a twelfth-century font with four curious-looking animals carved around its base; knowledgeable readers will no doubt pity my ignorance in thinking they might be otters. Later I looked them up and found that they were of course salamanders, emblems of baptism.

# 10

# The North-East Corner

HURST GREEN is a fair-sized main-road village, most of the buildings on the A21 being of nineteenth- or twentieth-century origin, although there are older ones at the west and along the A265 Lewes Road, which forms a junction with the A21 in the village centre. There is also a converted oast house, complete with cowl, at the north end, from which are sold fruit and vegetables, seven days a week, winter and summer. The little red-brick church of Holy Trinity lies back from the main road between a row of weather-boarded cottages and the Woolpack Inn, and dates from 1884. Its first full-time vicar was appointed in 1908 at a salary of £238. Hurst Green's chief benefactors were Lord Boyle, who gave the vicarage and the recreation ground, and Mrs Orme Carter who in 1906 provided £250 for oak stalls in the church and the decoration of the walls of Holy Trinity Church with a beautifully painted decorative frieze some six feet wide. Mrs Carter's gift was a memorial to her husband and her nineteen-year-old daughter.

Ticehurst, like all the villages in this part of Sussex and Kent, abounds with tile-hung and weather-boarded houses and cottages. Many date back to the eighteenth century and earlier, but there is a group of very recent weather-boarded houses at the south end opposite the Gothic revival Ticehurst Institute of 1899. *Hyrst* is the old English word for wooded height, *ticen* the Old English for kid or young goat, and in the first recorded reference to the village in 1180 it is spelt Tychenherste. The second part is still an accurate description of Ticehurst's setting, but we can only guess at the origins of the first. The oldest part of the oldest building in the village, the church of St Mary, goes back to the thirteenth century. Most of the rest is of fourteenth-century origin, although there have been many restorations, the most recent involving major repairs to the stonework and roof, treatment of the timbers, and redecoration. This began in 1970 and has cost some £10,000, much of the money being raised by public appeal. In a glass-fronted case inside the church is an embroidered smock of the type worn by farm labourers throughout Sussex until the early years of this century. It dates from around 1938, the inscription beneath it recording that it "represents much perfect work produced in past years by the Women's Institute smocking industry". The Courthorpe Chapel takes its name from a local family whose connections with Ticehurst go back over 400 years. Their home, Whiligh, midway between Ticehurst and Wadhurst, dates from 1586, and in the grounds there is an oak tree which is said to be over 2,000 years old. A companion was felled in the fourteenth century and used in the making of Westminster Hall.

It is very difficult to decide whether Wadhurst is a town or a village. Many books refer to it as a village but the parish magazine has a section entitled "Town in Focus" and with its many shops, large number of garages, schools—both state and fee-paying—railway, fire and police stations, two Brownie packs, British Legion, WRVS, Toc H, Youth Centre and Library it boasts a good many more amenities than are usually found in even the largest village. Architecturally it is well endowed, with a particularly attractive group of houses, cottages, inns and shops around the fine, large, parish church of St Peter and St Paul. This, like St Mary's, Ticehurst, which it resembles, dates chiefly from the thirteenth and fourteenth centuries.

The iron industry flourished in this hilly, densely wooded district. There are some forty iron grave-slabs in the churchyard, whilst tradition has it that the foundry at Lamberhurst, some four miles distant just across the Kent border, supplied the railings for St Paul's Cathedral churchyard.

The B2090, which links Hurst Green, Ticehurst and Wadhurst, comes to an end at the junction with the A267 Eastbourne to Tunbridge Wells road immediately south of Frant. Frant is less than three miles from Tunbridge Wells and inevitably the Kent spa is a social and shopping centre for many of the villages in this north-east corner of the county. This is not to say that they are mere appendages of it and generate no life of their own, but a good many inhabitants of Frant, which is a large village with some fine houses, work in Tunbridge Wells, and in Tonbridge and London.

This is still very much iron-working country and the pillars supporting the roof of the nave of the parish church of St Alban, Frant, are of Sussex iron. The church was almost entirely rebuilt in 1821, although there are some relics of earlier times including three cast-iron tomb slabs of 1631. The fifteenth-century Flemish stained glass also survived the rebuilding only to be largely destroyed when a flying bomb fell in the churchyard in 1944. Although it seems hard to believe, no less than sixteen such bombs exploded in and around the village. One landed on the village school at Tidebrook, two miles south-west of Wadhurst. Fortunately it was empty at the time and no one was hurt, but the school was never rebuilt. A plaque in the church records the event in the following words: "With thanksgiving to God for the preservation of the teachers and all the scholars of Tidebrook church school on 4th August, 1944 when an enemy flying bomb shattered the school buildings. Honour to discipline." Tidebrook children now go to Wadhurst and a house stands on the site. The church, a few yards below where the school used to stand, remains undamaged. It was built in 1856 and stands in a lush wooded valley and consequently Tidebrook has a very Gothic atmosphere.

Tidebrook lies midway between Wadhurst and Mayfield. The latter is yet another hilltop village and surely one of the most picturesque in all England. None of the approaches to it is disappointing, but the best involves turning off either the Tunbridge

Wells or Crowborough roads a mile to the north-west of Mayfield and ascending a steep lane to Argos Hill. At the top is a restored post-mill and opposite is a gate. From this gate there are magnificent views to be had across the Weald to the east, south and west, that to the south-east being dominated by the rooftops of Mayfield. Due east stands Pugin's Mayfield College and beyond that the wooded ridge amongst which are glimpses of Wadhurst, the most prominent being the spire of the parish church, Ridge upon wooded ridge extends southwards and westwards, with the barer slopes of Ashdown Forest and the South Downs amongst them. Due south of Mayfield is the high television mast at Cross-in-Hand, the only discernible twentieth-century structure. Because Argos Hill is away, although hardly remote, from main roads, it is little visited. Yet the view from it is such that one may admire it for hours, watching the infinite variety of greens, whatever the season, darken and lighten as the clouds pass over, picking out flashes of light reflected from car windscreens if it happens to be a sunny day, or the wisps of smoke rising from cottage chimneys hidden amongst the woods if it is a cold one, listening to the cows on the other side of the gate munching the grass, or the distant rumble of traffic climbing the hill into Mayfield. Sometimes there will be the more distinct sound of a tractor at work somewhere down below or of a light aeroplane passing over, perhaps from Biggin Hill, 10 minutes' flying time away, the drone of its piston engine recalling the autumn of 1940 when Argos Hill provided a grandstand for the Battle of Britain.

The most prominent building in Mayfield, seen from Argos Hill, is the college, now a girls' school and once a palace belonging to the Archbishops of Canterbury. St Dunstan is said to have been the first archbishop to live in Mayfield, in the tenth century, and to have built a wooden church on the hilltop. Its successor was burnt down in 1389 and replaced by one in the Perpendicular style, although the Early English tower, with a later shingled spire, survives. The church is called St Dunstan's, a dedication made shortly after the archbishop's death in 988. Mayfield was

one of the many Sussex parishes belonging to Godwin, his successor, as Domesday records, being the Earl of Mortain.

The fire of 1389 destroyed not only nearly all the church, but
also most of the houses in the villages and as a consequence many
of those in the main street today date from the early fifteenth
century. With the increase in population in Victorian times a
number of villages or hamlets around Mayfield became parishes in
their own right—Hadlow Down, Tidebrook, Mark Cross and Burwash Weald—and it was also at this time that the 1,000-year-old
direct link with Canterbury ended, Mayfield becoming a part of the
Diocese of Chichester. The finest surviving part of the Archbishop's Palace which Cranmer ceded to Henry VIII is the Medieval
Hall. It is now the school chapel, the largest part of the school
occupying buildings dating from the end of the nineteenth century.

Throughout the nineteenth century one family, the Kirbys, provided all the vicars of the parish. The first, the Rev. John Kirby
who came to Mayfield in 1780, was by all accounts a generous
man but a good deal too fond of drinking. The parishioners had
him removed in 1810, but obviously bore the family no ill will,
for they were happy to have his son as successor. He was of some
considerable comfort to them during the times of poverty and un-
rest following the Napoleonic Wars, and when he died in 1844 his
son, Henry Thomas Kirby, became vicar, at the age of twenty-
seven. As popular as his father and grandfather, he was also a
landowner of some standing. He farmed 400 acres, including some
hop fields, and the guide to the parish church records that he once
discovered a tramp in one of his barns suffering from smallpox
and personally nursed him back to health. Henry Thomas Kirby
served Mayfield for fifty-two years, longer than any other vicar,
and when he died his son, the last of the family and the third
John, took over. He carried on the family tradition of serving the
village, donating the village hall and the lancet window of St
Dunstan in the church. With his resignation due to ill health in
1912, the Kirby connection with Mayfield ended.

A narrow lane opposite the former palace leads down past

houses and cottages picturesquely sited on the hillside, out of the village, and along the valley of the Rother, to the B2181 Burwash Common to Wadhurst road at the hamlet of Witherenden Hill. A little north of Witherenden Hill it passes over the London to Hastings railway line beside Stonegate Station, and at Stonegate itself, a hamlet a mile up the road, a turning to the right leads by a somewhat devious route to Etchingham. The railway provides a much more direct route and a ride in the buffet car of one of the hourly trains which connects Frant, Wadhurst, Stonegate, Etchingham, Robertsbridge, Battle and Crowhurst with London, Tunbridge Wells and Hastings is a civilized and relaxing introduction to the villages and the countryside of East Sussex.

Etchingham is quite a small village, unusual in this part of Sussex in that it is set low down, beside the meeting of the Rivers Dudwell and Rother, and the fields around are thus subject to flooding. The church, at the east end of the village, is of great interest. It was built in the middle of the fourteenth century in the Decorated style by Sir William Echyngham (although the church guide refers to him as the "rebuilder"), and is little altered since that time. Its most prominent feature is its central tower, with iron strengthening pieces put in during the 1920s when it was in danger of collapse. Above is the weather-vane, made of copper in the form of the Echyngham Arms. It is contemporary with the rest of the church and is said to be the oldest weather-vane in England. If one happens to view it on a clear day, then one sees it as the designer intended, the sky forming the azure background to the Echyngham Arms. Equally ancient, the oldest in Sussex in fact, is the memorial brass to Sir William, recording his building of the church and his death in 1388. The only hints of a church older than Sir William's are some fragments of early fourteenth-century stained glass, found in the churchyard and placed in the east window of the north chapel in 1931, an exterior doorway on the south side with a trefoil pointed head, and the base of the font which is made of Purbeck marble.

Immediately west of the church the road makes a right-angle

turn and then begins to climb through the mixture of tile-hung, weather-boarded and modern buildings of the village, past a gateway to a wood and a sign saying "Beware of the Adders", and on to Kipling's village of Burwash.

Burwash, of course, had been in existence for over 1,000 years and was already regarded as worth a visit on account of its picturesqueness before Kipling moved into Batemans, a former ironmaster's house, down the hill from the main street, in 1902. But it is with him that the village is today chiefly associated. He lived in Burwash for thirty-four years, until his death in 1936 and in 1940 his widow bequeathed their house to the National Trust. Built in 1634, Batemans has been described as the "loveliest small house in Sussex". It is a very large small house, built of stone, set in extensive grounds opposite a field containing some of the friendliest and best-fed donkeys in the county, and much of it, including the study, is just as Kipling left it.

Kipling moved to Burwash from Rottingdean, to escape the crowds of admirers and sightseers which congregated there. On the whole he found the peace he was looking for, although inevitably the odd cranks appeared, including a particularly lunatic group who set up what they called a Kipling room in a local inn and expressed the hope that if the name stuck future generations might come to believe that the writer had actually worked there. The villagers came to know Kipling as a retiring, kindly man. P. G. Maude-Roxby recalls being allowed, as a small boy, to fish with his friends in the River Dudwell which runs through the grounds of Batemans, and being told stories by Kipling which were later published. This was in the years immediately after World War I: the name of Kipling's only son John is one of a hundred recorded on the Burwash War Memorial which Kipling unveiled. John was killed at Loos in August 1918, six weeks after his eighteenth birthday. When Kipling went abroad he used to send postcards back to the village boys who fished in his garden. He loved gadgets and Maude-Roxby one day found him trying out the hose of a new fire engine on the roof of Batemans. Several tiles were knocked off by the force of the water, which thrilled Kipling. At this time there were no street lights in Burwash and a lantern was set up in the War Memorial Tower and shone on the anniversary of the death of one of the village soldiers, sailors or airmen. The only other light in the village came from a beacon across the Kent border at Cranbrook, set up in the early 1930s to guide aircraft flying between Croydon and the Continent.

Burwash was rich in characters at this time. There was Cissy, a shepherdess who worked with her father, a middle-aged widower, tending flocks in the district. Like many people who work in the open air she was an unusually heavy sleeper. One night a strong wind blew in a window 8 feet by 6 feet in their cottage, but although she was only in the next room she continued to sleep soundly and did not discover the damage until the morning. At the age of twenty-seven she left the village to take charge of a large flock in Wales. Then there was the sexton, Arthur Richardson, who used to travel round the district learning folk songs from the locals. The village schoolmaster, Mr Verrall, would put them to music and they would then record them.

In the churchyard at Burwash is the oldest known Sussex iron grave-slab, belonging to an ironfounder who died in the fourteenth century. The houses and cottages in the main street, set close together, are of many styles, although inevitably there is a good deal which is tile-hung or weather-boarded. The overall effect is very fine, but it is unfortunate that the trees in front of them have of late been so hacked about. They present a very sad appearance, especially in winter when there are no leaves to hide their wounds.

Immediately south of Burwash are Netherfield, Brightling and Dallington. The former is an iron-working village with a long history, even though its church goes back no more than a hundred or so years; it was one of the settlements attacked by Norman skirmishing parties immediately before the Battle of Hastings. Dallington, set on a hilltop like Netherfield on the B2096 Heathfield to Battle road, has a parish church with a rare stone spire.

It is said that 'Mad' or 'Honest' Jack Fuller of Brightling wagered he could see this spire from his house and when he found he couldn't, he had a copy put up at Brightling a mile away to fool his opponent.

Fuller was a true eccentric, his character a mixture of impetuosity, shrewdness, good humour and benevolence. He is chiefly remembered for his crazy architectural excesses, the imitation spire being but one. He built an obelisk on the top of the 647-foot Brightling Down in the shape of a tall needle, and in the grounds of Brightling Park he had erected an artificial stone summerhouse and a temple. Outside he had an observatory put up on the road to Woods Corner, but weirdest of all was a triangular mausoleum in the churchyard. He had himself buried in this, wrapped in an iron chain, and broken glass was strewed outside so that "when the devil comes to claim his own he might at least cut his feet".

But it may not have been the Devil who came for Jack Fuller when he died in 1833, for although he was opposed to the abolition of slavery on account of the estates he owned in Jamaica, he once rode all the way from Brightling to Westminster, simply to call the speaker "the insignificant little fellow in the wig", was thrown out of the House by the Sergeant-at-Arms and rode straight home again, and spent £20,000 getting himself re-elected to Parliament in 1807. He also had a high wall several miles long built around his estate to provide work for the local unemployed—one of the motives, perhaps, behind his follies—commissioned Turner to do five pictures in the district, refused a peerage from Pitt declaring "I was born Jack Fuller and Jack Fuller I'll die", saved Bodiam Castle from demolition, gave £10,000 to the Royal Institution of Great Britain and founded two scholarships. His family had made their money from ironworking and from their Jamaican estates—his house, Rose Hill, was named after his grandmother Elizabeth Rose of Jamaica—and he never married.

From Brightling a series of lanes leads up to the A265 Hurst Green to Uckfield Road at Burwash Common, a large hamlet once notorious for smugglers and sheep stealers. The A265 continues along a high ridge through Broad Oak to Heathfield and thence to the A267 Eastbourne to Tunbridge Wells road and the busy crossroads at Cross-in-Hand. North of this is the straggling hamlet of Five Ashes. The main road swings right here towards Mayfield but a byroad continues due north to Rotherfield. This is a handsome, quiet village, within sight of Jarvis Brook on the eastern edge of the great sprawl of Crowborough, but sufficiently far away and above it to be quite separate and remote. The road from Five Ashes joins that from Mayfield at the southern end of the main street, makes a right-angled turn in the village centre at the junction of the Wadhurst and Eridge Roads, and continues on past the church on the left, the post office on the right, down the hill towards Jarvis Brook. At the bottom of the hill a turning to the right leads to a ford through a tributary of the Ouse. Fords are rare in Sussex, the only other one I know in the locality being through another tributary of the Ouse at Herons Ghyll on the southern edge of the Ashdown Forest.

The parish church of Rotherfield has the unusual name of St Denys. The first church of St Denys was built towards the end of the eighth century by Bertwald, a Saxon Duke who owned a great deal of land around where Rotherfield now stands. He had gone to the monastery of St Denys near Paris for a cure and in thanksgiving erected the church, at the same time establishing a monastery of St Denys nearby. The harbours at Hastings and Pevensey were bequeathed for the monastery's maintenance. There is no positive record of where the monastery stood, although there are clues in the village. There is, for example, a Chant Lane, which it is suggested takes its name from the chanting monks making their way to the priory church, and there is a pond which may once have supplied the monks with fish. The priory was disbanded around the time of the Conquest, the lands probably becoming the property of the crown for it is known that William Rufus hunted at Rotherfield.

The present church dates chiefly from the thirteenth century, although there is a good deal of a later date, including a very fine fifteenth-century ceiling in the Nevill chapel embossed with grotesque heads and the Tudor rose and portcullis badges of the Nevill family, a fifteenth-century shingled steeple which was extensively refurbished some ten years ago, and the east window which was designed by Burne Jones and made by the William Morris Company. There are extensive remains of frescoes dating from the thirteenth, fourteenth and fifteenth centuries, one of which, painted around 1430, depicts two monks and would suggest that the priory was still in existence at this time. There is a panoramic picture of Rotherfield, which may or may not be very exact, painted in 1711 and hanging in the church which depicts ruins which could be those of the monastery.

The Nevill family and their descendants the Abergavennys have been associated with this part of Sussex for the best part of 1,000 years; they came over with the Conqueror and have owned land in the district since then, the family seat being at Eridge. Eridge Castle, built in 1787, was extensively rebuilt in 1938–9 and since 1955 part of it has contained a Museum of Costume, a very large collection of clothes dating from the middle of the eighteenth century onwards; there is also a fashion research centre. Early in 1938 the Marquess of Abergavenny was thrown from his horse whilst out riding in the castle grounds and killed. He was eighty-three and had been heard to say he wished to die whilst out hunting, so presumably his end was not regarded as a tragic one. Eridge itself consists of two sections, neither really big enough to call itself a village. At the southern end there is the railway station and a mile up the road towards Tunbridge Wells is Eridge Green, which, with its very Gothic-looking church of Holy Trinity and a few houses, is a little bit more substantial.

Groombridge, the next station up the line towards Tunbridge Wells, really belongs to Kent, all, that is, except for the newer suburban bit and the station which are in Sussex. Between Eridge and Groombridge are Harrisons Rocks, an outcrop of the Hastings Sand belt. They are some 30 to 40 feet high, smoothed and shaped by rain and frost, and provide ideal practice for rock climbers. They have been so used since the middle of the nineteenth century but only became really well known around 1930 after being highly spoken of in a book issued by the Camping Clubs of Great Britain and Ireland. Easily reached from London—the railway line passes within sight of them—they became immensely popular and have remained so. A great many varieties of climbs are possible, difficult enough to provide practice even for Himalayan expeditions, but also suitable for beginners. The rocks are a great favourite with school parties and boys'—and girls'—clubs, and at weekends hundreds of young people can be seen walking from Groombridge Station and from car parks down through the woods to the rocks.

Ashurst, like Groombridge, is also partly in Kent, although the little church, dating from 1624, is in Sussex. There was a large corn watermill here on a branch of the Medway, which was at work until September 1930 when a severe fire virtually destroyed it, leaving only the gaunt skeleton of the iron wheel, 16 feet in diameter.

It is quite easy to drive through Withyham and not recognize it for a village at all. It lies on the B2110 Tunbridge Wells to Forest Row road and all one is aware of is a large public house, the Dorset Arms, and a small group of houses in a dip where the road curves round and crosses a stream, and some distance beyond this the church. It is not very difficult to miss this latter altogether for it is set high up above the road amongst trees, also on a bend and by a narrow bridge across another stream. From the bank on which St Michael and All Angels, Withyham, stands, one may see the spire of St Mary the Virgin, Hartfield, a mile away to the west. No one could doubt that Hartfield is a village with its substantial main street of weather-boarded, stone, brick and tile-hung cottages, a skilfully converted non-conformist chapel, shops, a second streeet also with a Dorset Arms leading to the church, and a second section of the village called Upper Hart-field, up the hill towards Forest Row. The correct postal address of Withyham is Withyham, Hartfield and one might be excused for assuming that the former was no more than an appendage of the latter. Yet if one did, one would be doing it a grave injustice as a delightful booklet on sale in Withyham church makes clear. Edited by I. R. S. Cosby with the assistance of many local people, in particular the Rev. Peter Scott, rector since 1953, it records with humour and insight the life and times of a community rich in character and variety, and I gratefully acknowledge the permission of Mr Cosby and the Rev. Scott to extract information and to quote from it.

In the earliest records, 1095, the village is called Wideham, and in the twelfth century a female descendant of Robert de Dene, chief butler of William the Conqueror who owned much of Withyham in succession to the Conqueror's half brother, Robert Earl of Morteyn, married Sir Jordain de Sackville. The present-day significance of this marriage 800 years ago is that the Sackville family still owns land in Withyham. Indeed the visitor to the church is almost overwhelmed by the monuments to elevated and famous people within it. The best-known of recent years is that to the poetess Victoria Sackville West who died in 1967 and whose ashes lie at Withyham. A second memorial dating from that year is to the cabinet minister, Maxwell Fyfe. The grandest of all the memorials is the Sackville one of the late seventeenth century with its life-size figures carved by Cibber and erected as part of the restoration programme after the church had been struck by lightning and almost destroyed in 1663.

Withyham is as peaceful and as strategically useless a place as one could imagine, yet the wars of this century have not left it unscathed. Fifteen Withyham men including the head of the Sackvilles, the 8th Earl De La Warr, died in World War I. Three died in the Services between 1939 and 1945 and during that time a number of bombs dropped in the fields and woods of Withyham, the church twice suffering blast damage. In September 1940 Spitfires, Hurricanes, Dorniers, Messerschmitts and Heinkels wheeled above Withyham, Hartfield and the surrounding parishes as the Battle of Britain was fought. Troops were stationed in considerable numbers in the area and five German airmen and a Czech soldier were buried in the churchyard although their remains have since been moved elsewhere. The only visible relics of the two world wars remaining today are the war memorials and a blockhouse in a field near the church.

For exactly 100 years Withyham and Hartfield each had railway stations, on the single-track line which connected Tunbridge Wells with East Grinstead and thence London. In a collection of reminiscences put together by the Withyham Women's Institute in the mid 1950s an old lady, Mrs Coomber, recalled travelling on the first train which "rushed through Withyham Station, and Hartfield too, and did not stop until Forest Row was reached. The reason remains unknown". Ironically the man chiefly responsible for the closing of the line, Dr Beeching, lived near Forest Row and regularly travelled up to London on the line when he was Chairman of British Railways in the early 1960s. Withyham Station was actually in a district known as Balls Green in the northern part of the parish and with the coming of the railway a number of houses and a school were built there. All these remain, including the station, although it is now derelict. Hartfield Station has suffered a happier fate for it has become a play centre, Jenny Agutter, the star of *The Railway Children*, coming down to inaugurate work on it, and much has since been done although it is not yet completely renovated.

The grandest building in the district is Buckhurst Park, home of the Sackvilles, which stands behind the church and on the slopes of the Ashdown Forest. It dates from 1690, replacing Buckhurst House which lay to the west and stood on a side occupied at least as far back as Domesday. This latter was abandoned when Knole, near Sevenoaks, came into the family in 1603. A year later Thomas Sackville became Earl of Dorset (hence the Dorset Arms in Withyham and Hartfield); the De La Warr title entered the family in the nineteenth century when the 5th Duke of Dorset died and was succeeded by his sister, Countess De La Warr. Buckhurst House is now a ruin, the largest surviving section being a stone gatehouse.

M

Buckhurst Park was enlarged at various times during the eighteenth and nineteenth centuries and in the first decade of the present century a wing designed by Lutyens was added, but this was pulled down by the present Lord Buckhurst, elder son of Earl De La Warr, who is the present occupier of Buckhurst Park. The parish of Withyham is extensive and stretches some seven miles in all from north to south, from the Kent border to the heart of the Ashdown Forest, and embraces, apart from those already mentioned, the communities of Blackham, Lye Green, Mott's Mill, Summerhales Hill, Withyham St John's and Friars Gate. To its south-east lies the sprawling town of Crowborough, whilst along the whole of its southern border, and that of Hartfield, is the Ashdown Forest. Turner, who painted so much in Sussex, paid his first visit to the county in 1793 at the age of eighteen when he came to Withyham, although it is not recorded that he did any work here. A perhaps less permanently famous artist, Brian Jones of the Rolling Stones, has tragic associations with the area for he died in the swimming pool of a house in Hartfield. A. A. Milne also lived in Hartfield and wrote many of the Pooh stories at his home in the village, and the great authority on Roman roads in the south-east of England, Ivan D. Margary, has a house here. He was largely responsible for the discovery of the Roman road which passes right through Hartfield.

The existence of this London to Lewes road was known but not its precise location until Margary started his investigations. In 1929 he had the Ashdown Forest photographed from the air and the pictures resulting revealed the straight, parallel lines he had been looking for. He then began excavations and over the years established the route with some precision. The most exciting section for the layman is that by Holtye Common, a mile or so north of Hartfield. Margary excavated this in 1939, got down to the actual metalling and even revealed wheel-marks. This remarkable state of preservation is due to the iron cinders of the surface fusing and rusting together to form a hard, unyielding mass. Margary presented his excavated section of road to the Sussex

Archaeological Society and it remains visible to the public who may visit it by taking the signposted footpath just east of Holtye Common on the A264 East Grinstead–Tunbridge Wells road and following it down the hill until the exposed, fenced-off Roman road is reached. The footpath continues along the line of the road into Hartfield. Further evidence of the road can be found up on the forest ridge beyond Hartfield close to the modern B2026 Westerham to Haresfield road, and in the other direction, across the Kent border it forms the B2026, itself on a perfectly straight alignment of some two miles through Edenbridge.

The iron cinders which formed the surface of the Roman road are a reminder of the iron industry which flourished hereabouts. It was active before Roman times and continued until the eighteenth century. The remains are numerous, although not easy to trace, and one needs the standard work on the subject, Ernest Straker's *Wealden Iron*, when attempting to find them. The last active ironworks in the district would seem to have been that at Scarlets, beside the sixteenth-century house of that name, on the banks of the Kent Water which divides Sussex and Kent, and is also less than a mile from Surrey. It ceased working some time in the middle of the eighteenth century and was one of the last surviving furnaces in the whole of the Weald. Less than a mile east is the site of the Cowden furnace, the mill being in Kent, the wheel which powered the bellows of the furnace being in Sussex. A cannon was dug up on the site around 1850 and the pond which provided the water may still be seen. It covers some 30 acres and is known as the Furnace Pond. As it is in Kent I suppose we shouldn't really mention it, but at least it can be seen from Sussex. A former Sussex hammerpond is that in Buckhurst Park, south-east of Withyham church. It is much altered from the mid-seventeenth century when the furnace last worked and is now an ornamental lake in the grounds of the house.

The Sussex portions of the Scarlets and Cowden furnaces lie in the parish of Hammerwood and Holtye, north of Hartfield. The former name is the clearest indication of the villages' origins, if village it can be called. There are no shops, unless one counts a garden and vegetable centre, but there is a church beside the East Grinstead–Tunbridge Wells road and the man mowing the grass in the churchyard assured me that Hammerwood was a village. The church at Hammerwood is certainly the most noticeable building in the vicinity, for it stands in isolation on a ridge with fine views to the north and south. It was built in 1879 and is used in conjunction with St Peter's, Holtye, which antedates it by thirteen years. It is not normally open except when services are in progress, a situation which dates from the occasion when one of the ornate iron candelabra was stolen; fortunately a replacement was available. Amongst the memorial plaques are two to members of the Whidborne family, who were once prominent in the district. Both were called George Ferris Whidborne. The father was a former vicar of St George's, Battersea, and died at Hammerwood in 1910; the son died of wounds in France in 1915. The parish war memorial is at the west corner of the extensive Holtye Common; further along is the church, whilst at the east end is the White Horse Inn where guide books to the Roman road excavations can usually be bought.

There were forges active in Hammerwood and Holtye until the middle of the seventeenth century, and in a sense the industry has never died, for although iron has not been mined in Sussex for some 150 years, ironworks and blacksmiths' shops still exist. Mr Reddick, a blacksmith who works just across the Surrey border in Dormansland, has a collection of Sussex iron firebacks and takes a great interest in the history of his industry. He was apprenticed on leaving school in 1945 and has a great many stories to tell which he heard from old blacksmiths. One fact he related which does not seem to be generally known is that after prohibitions had been placed on the use of local wood for fuel, coal was used. Guns made in the Forest Row and East Grinstead districts passed through Dormans on their way to Woolwich and the horse-drawn wagons which conveyed them returned loaded with coal from colliers in the Thames.

Forest Row, together with Ashurst Wood, which form one parish, is now virtually linked to East Grinstead, a ribbon of development stretching up to the lower northern slopes of the Ashdown Forest and served by London Country buses from Croydon. The church, like those at Holtye and Hammerwood, dates from the nineteenth century; two miles away at Colemans Hatch on the Forest Row–Hartfield road there is an even more modern one, built in 1913, and until Victorian times the parish churches of East Grinstead, Hartfield and Withyham sufficed for the entire district bounded by the Kent border on the north, the southern slopes of the Ashdown Forest to the south, East Grinstead to the west and Tunbridge Wells to the east.

Forest Row has gone on developing down to the present day, a consequence of its position on the A22 London to Eastbourne road. There is a new estate to the west of the road but the largest part of the village is to the east, stretching up the slopes of the forest and along the Hartfield road for some considerable distance. It is largely residential and people commute to London, although the closure of the station means they now have to motor to East Grinstead. The only industrial site of any significance is a large timber-yard which used to stand beside the station; it now finds itself a neighbour of the local Conservative Club, a social club, the fire station and the council depot.

One cannot but be aware of the influence of the Freshfield family upon Forest Row. The family seat of Kidbrooke Park, an early eighteenth-century house with additions, lies to the south-west of the village on the road to West Hoathly. The mock Tudor hall which stands in the centre of Forest Row, across the road from the church, was erected by Henry Ray Freshfield in 1898, and inside the church is a monument to Henry Doyles Freshfield who died seven years earlier at the age of thirteen. Nowadays the people of Forest Row depend more on each other rather than on the benevolence of wealthy local landowners; they have formed a 'Good Neighbours' group, and list amongst its services "driving, shopping, hospital visiting, general visiting, emergency needs and emergency childminding". In times when public transport in country areas is so much poorer than it used to be but when there are so many more cars about, mothers of small children and elderly people find such assistance invaluable.

North of Forest Row the A22 makes a reverse curve away to the west to avoid Ashurstwood, passing an opening which leads down to the ruins of Brambletye, a four-storey mansion built in 1631. The old road leads straight up a steep hill into Ashurstwood, past a blacksmith's shop which stands beside Hammerwood Road; perhaps the iron village sign was made here. Ashurstwood is part village, part suburb, largely Victorian and later, belonging to the parish of Forest Row, although it has a church of its own—Christ Church, built in 1884—and a United Reformed church, and tends to look towards East Grinstead, which begins where it ends, for most of its needs.

It stands in a high position, looking southwards across the valley in which Forest Row lies to the still higher Ashdown Forest, whilst northwards East Grinstead slopes gently away beyond the trees.

There are two principal routes linking East Grinstead and Crawley, by way either of Copthorne or Turners Hill; both are well used, particularly the former, which passes for some of its distance through Surrey. The latter is much the most attractive with some fine views, particularly in the vicinity of Turners Hill. When it was decided after World War II to erect a new town at Crawley a good deal of care was taken in its planning, but although this care is evident today throughout Crawley, it is obvious that less thought was given to what would happen to the villages around. As a consequence some of them have acquired a suburban air, with filling stations which serve the needs of the passing motorists but look out of place in a rural area. There are housing developments which owe more to the presence of Crawley than to the original needs of the village, and the result is something which is neither village, nor town, nor country.

Felbridge is really a Surrey village, situated at the junction of the A22 and the A264 East Grinstead to Crawley roads, but it spills over into Sussex. Copthorne, midway along the A264, belongs to Sussex but spills over into Surrey. It has a Victorian church, a lot of fairly recent building, and one of the dedicated Leonard Cheshire's homes for the disabled. The next village along the road, Pound Hill, was absorbed into Crawley in the early 1950s, but to the north, maintaining a precarious independence beside Gatwick Airport, is Tinsley Green. Here, at The Greyhound, the annual marbles championships are held on each Good Friday. These go back to 1630 and attract contestants from all over the country, some of whom take it all very seriously, some of whom go along just for the fun and the publicity. The championships died out around 1900 but were revived in the 1930s, at which time one Sam Spooner, a champion of the 1890s, was still playing with his original marbles. He had presumably not broken the rule which decrees that those who have not finished their game by noon have their marbles confiscated and stamped into the ground.

Crawley Down is a mile and a half south of Copthorne on the B2028, one of a number of useful secondary north-to-south roads which never suffer the congestion which sometimes afflicts the A22 and the A23. Crawley Down is a modern, sprawling development which partly owes its existence to the now vanished Grange Road station which used to be served by East Grinstead to Three Bridges trains. A mile further south is Turners Hill. This is a much older place, a village high on a ridge and for long an important crossing place of north-to-south and east-to-west routes. The B2028 sweeps round beside a nicely laid out council estate and then climbs up to the crossroads. The main street containing a number of tile-hung cottages branches off to the right and is therefore conveniently free of through traffic, and the yellowish-grey stone church of St Leonard, dating from the last decade of the nineteenth century, is at the top of it and to the right, at the very highest point of the ridge. From it one may look northwards into Surrey to the white landmark of the Oxted chalkpits out into the North Downs, and southwards to the South Downs and Ditchling

Beacon. Within the parish there is the appropriately named Hill Top Women's Institute. Three miles west of Turners Hill and very nearly part of Crawley is Worth. The Priory on the ridge to the south of the village contains Paddockhurst, a very large mock Tudor mansion built in 1869–72. At the end of the nineteenth century it belonged to Robert Whitehead, the inventor of the torpedo, and he used the rock-garden pool at the house for his experiments. He was originally a textile machinery engineer and unlike many men who hit upon a new idea he made a great deal of money out of his. He worked for a time in Milan where he became a friend of Garibaldi, and he moved on from there to Austria, Germany and Turkey. Whitehead received £15,000 from the British Government, whilst his connections with the rulers of Europe enabled his family to contract some highly advantageous marriages. His daughter became the wife of an Austrian count and a granddaughter married Bismarck's son. So opulent was life at Paddockhurst at this time and during the period of Whitehead's successor, Sir Weetman Pearson, that there was a separate chapel for the staff and a hen house designed by Lutyens with a parquet floor. Pearson sold Paddockhurst to Downside School for its preparatory department.

Set between the B2036 and the London to Brighton motorway is one of the finest churches in all England. The parish church of St Nicholas, Worth, is largely Saxon with a virtually original tenth- or eleventh-century chancel and transepts and, in the words of the guidebook, "is the outstanding example of a Saxon church built on a cruciform plan with an apsidal chancel". Amongst its many items of architectural, historical and religious interest are an unusually large 22-foot-high chancel arch, various other Saxon features including high entrance archways by the south door and the now built up north one, three twin-arched light windows, a processional cross dating from 1519 brought over from Bruges, a pulpit of 1577 from Worth in Germany, and a thirteenth-century font. At the west end of the nave is a gallery of 1610 with a handsome nineteenth-century stained-glass window behind. This is the

least Saxon part of the church but it is nevertheless very attractive;
I visited it one winter afternoon when the choir was at practice
and the scene, with the reds of the choristers' cassocks, the dark
brown of the woodwork and the yellow of the filtering light
through the window was reminiscent of a Breughel painting.

Worth is our last Sussex village, and in a tour which has so often
taken us to the parish church where much of the history of the
community is enshrined, it is appropriate that we should end at a
church which transports us back one thousand years to the days
before the Norman Conquest and the beginnings of Sussex village
life.

# Index

188    INDEX

Pub George & Dragon at Dragon Green (near Bathes Green)

Memorial Tablee in Pub from his albino son -

same "beer sloshing" revived there now

Marly Robins Eerg (Country)